ANGLO-SAXON RIDDLES OF THE EXETER BOOK

anglo-saxon riddles of the exeter book

translated by

PAULL F. BAUM

DUKE UNIVERSITY PRESS

Durham, North Carolina

1 9 6 3

Printed in the United States of America
by the Seeman Printery, Inc., Durham, N. C.

PREFACE

THE ninety-odd riddles in Anglo-Saxon which have come down to us in a single manuscript are naturally a miscellaneous collection of varying merit. A few of them are poetical in the best sense of Anglo-Saxon poetic style, as good as anything outside the heroic style of the *Beowulf*. Many of them are interesting as riddles: intentional ambiguities to be solved by reader or hearer. Some of them are learned, turning on the interpretation of runic letters or dealing with subjects only the monkish mind would care about. Some of them are neat and clever and well versified; others are not so good.

In the manuscript the riddles appear in no particular order. The following translations have been grouped according to subject. It was not feasible to arrange them by types, because the typical forms of the riddle are not clearly fixed and the Anglo-Saxon riddles are too few to illustrate many types.

The language of the Anglo-Saxon riddles is often difficult, and even those who are fairly familiar with Old English cannot read them readily. Though some of the best have been translated in scattered places, and there is a prose line-for-line translation in the E.E.T.S. edition of the Exeter Book, not readily accessible to the common reader, it has seemed worthwhile to render them all in similar verse form, with brief explanations, for any who may be interested in the riddles as such and for the glimpses they afford of monkish diversion and of daily life in England of the eighth and ninth centuries—in modern terms, for their psychological and sociological values.

I am deeply indebted to Professor Elliott V. K. Dobbie for reading my manuscript with great care and suggesting many improvements.

P.F.B.

CONTENTS

INTRODUCTION

RIDDLES are, so to say, universal. Some are so widespread as to deserve the name of world-riddles. The same theme will appear in different places, at different times, with different treatment, either from a common origin scattered by oral or written transmission, or of spontaneous origin based on similar observation or similar mental processes.[1] Riddles appear in the Vedas and in the Koran. The Sphinx riddle is famous, and Homer is said to have died of vexation because he could not solve this one: "What we caught we threw away; what we could not catch we kept."[2] Samson propounded one to the Philistines on a wager: "Out of the eater came forth meat, and out of the strong came forth sweetness" (Judg. 14:12-14). The Philistines lost, and no wonder. One of the best-known riddles involving a gamble occurs in the incest story of Apollonius of Tyre, related by Gower (*Confessio Amantis* VIII, 271 ff.) and deplored by Chaucer.[3] (Our Riddle *46* is based on incest.)

Thus riddles exist on two levels, popular (oral) and literary (learned), often passing from one group to the other. For a folk riddle may be taken over by the learned and dressed accordingly, or vice versa, a learned riddle may pass to the folk and suffer modification to fit popular taste. Our Anglo-Saxon riddles illustrate both movements. No positive distinctions can be made, but in general the longer and more poetic may safely be called learned, notably the Storm riddles, but also for a different reason those containing runes; and

1. For a rich collection illustrating comparative riddle lore, see Archer Taylor, *English Riddles from Oral Transmission*, Berkeley, 1951.
2. The story is told in the Herodotean *Life of Homer*. The poet questioned some boys who had returned from fishing and was answered by the riddle. The answer is given in Symphosius 30, Pedunculus, 'louse.'
3. Apollonius asks for the hand of the daughter of the King of Antioch and is told that he must answer a riddle correctly or suffer death: "I have eaten my mother's flesh and now I seek my father, her husband who is also my wife's son." This has had a long history before and since Gower and is familiar from Shakespeare's *Pericles* (I, i, ll. 64-71). Another story in which a bride is won by answering a riddle is the ballad of Captain Wedderburn's Courtship (Child 46), which appears in literary form in Gozzi's *La Turandot*, translated by Schiller, and set to music by Puccini. In Child 1 the devil threatens to carry off a maiden if she cannot answer his seven riddles.

the shorter (and metrically inferior ones) must be regarded as popular, notably those on simple domestic themes and the so-called obscene riddles. Riddle 5 (K-D 84) may serve as an example of the crossing. "It is to be feared," says A. J. Wyatt, "that, after a secular youth, the riddle passed some time in a monastery."

. Riddles belong to that large family of expressions in which something is represented as something else, as in simile and metaphor. A resemblance is stated or implied and its significance is assumed to be more or less easily recognized—as when the camel is called the ship of the desert. But in the riddle there is introduced an element of calculated deception; the resemblance is submerged in deliberate ambiguity or obscurity. As in a detective story the clues are given but not made obvious. This ambiguity may take two forms. In one the riddler says, "I was not really trying to deceive you but only to test your agility and to share the satisfaction of deducing the answer." Such are the *Ænigmata* of Aldhelm. In the other, the riddler means to trick the hearer maliciously; he may force an ambiguity beyond the limits of fair play or he may possess special knowledge which others cannot be expected to have—as in Samson's riddle to the Philistines. The one is a good-natured exercise of intelligence; the other is a trial of wits, the riddler holding cards and spades and hoping to exhibit his superiority. The one is an epigram, the other a game. Then there may be a middle ground, when the honors are "easy" and the victim can retort that he was not honestly used and anyway by the stated terms there could be more than one legitimate answer. This leads to lively expostulation and reply. Sometimes the answer is concealed in words, as in 28 (K-D 13), Ten Chickens, or in signs, as in the runes. Sometimes there is word play: *weax* 76 (K-D 45, 1), *hafte* 48 (K-D 73, 22), *blæce* 56 (K-D 93, 24), and elsewhere. When the riddle is put into verse there is the increment of poetical language to heighten the ambiguity, or, on the other hand, the language may be strained to satisfy metrical requirements.

In quite another fashion the Anglo-Saxon riddler has an advantage over us, in that he knows the language better than we do and is familiar with many things which we are obliged to get up—as in the description of a primitive plow or weaver's loom. And finally, he had better texts.

The founder of riddling in England was Aldhelm (*ca.* 640-709), abbot of Malmesbury and later bishop of Sherborne, one of the most distinguished pupils of the great school of Canterbury. Under Irish influence (the abbey of Malmesbury was founded by the Irish scholar Maildubh) he cultivated an elaborate Latin style, which tends to obscure his great learning. In his prose work *Epistola ad Acircium* (695) he included one hundred *Ænigmata* in hexameters, ranging in length from four to eighty-three lines, on a great variety of subjects meant to glorify God's creation. They begin with Earth, Wind, Cloud, and other natural phenomena, and end fittingly with the longest, *Creatura*, or Creation. They are unlike riddles in that they do not pose a problem and ask for an answer, but are each headed by self-explanatory titles. Aldhelm acknowledges as his model the one hundred *Ænigmata* of one Symphosius (of uncertain date) about which nothing is known beyond his work.[4] Aldhelm was followed in England by Tatwine, archbishop of Canterbury (d. 734), and Eusebius, generally identified with Hwætberht, abbot of Wearmouth and a friend of Bede. Between them Tatwine and Eusebius produced another one hundred *Ænigmata*. Aldhelm is known to have composed poems in the vernacular, admired by King Alfred; and there is a story reported by William of Malmesbury (who had it from a lost work of King Alfred's) of how Aldhelm would stand at a bridge and by reciting like a minstrel hope to entice passersby into the church. Thus it would not be surprising if he had composed riddles in the vernacular, but none in the Exeter Book can be reasonably attributed to him—unless possibly the Storm riddles (see pp. 3-7 below). Riddles *11* (K-D 40) and *50* (K-D 35) are translations of Aldhelm.

The editors of the Exeter riddles have sedulously traced the parallels with these four Latin collections, but relatively few are close enough to show direct influence. Numbers *41* (K-D 60) and *42* (K-D 47) are from Symphosius and *62* (K-D 85) resembles one of his (Fish and

4. Aldhelm also remembered the passage in II Chron. 25:18 which tells cryptically how a king of Israel sent to a king of Judah saying, "The thistle that was in Lebanon sent to the cedar that was in Lebanon, saying Give thy daughter to my son to wife; and there passed by a wild beast that was in Lebanon, and trod down the thistle."

River). In some dozen and a half others there are fainter connec-
tions with the Latin riddles, different editors holding different views.
But the point is that these two hundred Latin enigmas must have
suggested the composition of vernacular riddles, most of them probably by clerics, in that transitional middle-world between pagan and
Christian, when those men who were sufficiently trained to write
English verse could look both ways and feel no hesitation in mingling
the sacred and profane. The same is true of the man who compiled
the Exeter Book.

MANUSCRIPT

Leofric, bishop of Exeter (d. 1072), gave to his cathedral library
"one large book in English verse on various subjects." This, the
Exeter Book, is a manuscript of 130 folios written in one hand, probably late in the tenth century. These various subjects are mostly re-
ligious, that is, either Christian or of markedly Christian coloring.
Among them are three poems—*Wanderer, Seafarer, Riming Poem*—
which are pagan elegies lamenting the degenerate times, but with
homiletic passages which are perhaps interpolations; and also half a
dozen pieces, running to more than 350 lines all together, which are
clearly Germanic pagan in origin. These are (to give them their
modern titles) *Widsith, Deor, Wulf and Eadwacer* (called sometimes
the *Quondam First Riddle* because the earliest editors mistook it for a
riddle), *The Wife's Lament, The Lover's Message,* and *The Ruin.*
   The Riddles come toward the end of the manuscript in three
places: beginning on fol. 101a, the first fifty-nine riddles; these are
followed by *The Wife's Lament* and seven other pieces; then a second
text of K-D 30 and K-D 60; then after *The Lover's Message* and *The
Ruin,* the remaining riddles, K-D 61-95. The last several folios of the
manuscript were at some time damaged, probably by fire, leaving the
text badly mutilated. It would seem therefore that the scribe had
before him first a group of fifty-nine riddles. Later he came upon,
or was given, another text of 30, which he copied without recognizing
or regardless of the repetition, and then followed it by 60, if that is
really a riddle (see pp. 33 f. below). Next he added two poems which

are not riddles. Finally he received a set of thirty-five riddles and added them. That the scribe simply copied down what came to him without thought of unity or coherence is apparent from the separation of the two monologues, *The Wife's Lament* and *The Lover's Message*, which are of the same type and possibly parts of the same story. It is apparent also that the riddles copied by the Exeter scribe were not a single collection of one hundred (matching the count of the Latin *Ænigmata* of Aldhelm and Tatwine-Eusebius); and this fact, along with the uncertainty in the editorial numbering of several and the inclusion of a Latin riddle, makes it hazardous to assume that there were originally one hundred Anglo-Saxon riddles.

TRANSLATION

The difficulties of translating Anglo-Saxon poetry are well known; the attempt to translate the Anglo-Saxon riddles faces several peculiar difficulties. The text is in many places corrupt, and while excellent scholars have worked it over they are often at variance even as to the literal meaning and they have sometimes emended in the interest of a favored solution. The words themselves can be deceptive. Such a simple word as "plow," for example, represents an object different from the modern reader's picture. Since it is the nature of a riddle to deal in ambiguities, a translator must somehow hold the line between revealing too much and preserving a necessary obscurity. And when there is no generally accepted solution, one must guard against slanting the translation toward one's own guess. Moreover, the riddles vary in merit. For the best of them one does one's best; for the others one tries not to make them appear better than the original. The result is, therefore, a series of compromises in the hope of achieving "the best possible failure." Finally, there is the question of metrical form. Modern imitations of the Anglo-Saxon long line of four main stresses, with two, often three, alliterating syllables to the line, have usually been unsatisfactory. Hence in the following versions I have settled for a loose line, generally of four stresses, with as much alliteration as comes without forcing—a middle ground between strict meter and rhythmic prose, avoiding, or at least diminishing, the iambic movement which has dominated English verse for so long, which our ear has lately learned to do without and which the Anglo-Saxon ear never knew.

Although there are several translations of selected riddles,[5] there has hitherto been no English translation of all the Exeter Book riddles except that of Professor W. S. Mackie in the E.E.T.S. edition (London, 1934), a line-by-line rendering aimed primarily at accuracy and clearness.

A close look at two specimens will best illustrate the problems and the present method.

First, riddle 26 (K-D 38), Bull Calf, is comparatively simple. It consists of seven lines which correspond roughly to the six hexameters of Aldhelm's *De Bovo, sive Juvenco*: "Slaking the dryness of my mouth with foaming throat I thirstily drew in my drink from twice two throats. While living I break up the fertile clods of soil along with the stubble by the effort of my stout strength; but when the breath leaves my chill frame, I can bind men fast in terrible bonds" (Wyatt's translation). The Anglo-Saxon expands the first two hexameters into four lines and compresses the remaining four hexameters into three epigrammatic lines. It is bare where the Latin is flowery, but it has its own kind of indirection at the beginning. It runs: "I saw the creature [*wiht* is a feminine noun and thus misleading about the gender of the solution; so it adds at once] of the weaponed-kind [i.e., a male creature, one which fights with weapons, to be later recognized as the animal's horns], eager for the joys of youth [suggesting the sexual urge, but this is at once corrected]. It lets for its use [literally, for tribute] four life-giving fountains brightly shoot, gush forth, to its delight [*on gesceap* is uncertain; it may mean 'as fate wills']. [With a different punctuation the sense would be: 'the life-sustainer (mother, cow) lets four fountains. . . .'] A man spake [*maðelode*, a word from the epic style] who said to me: 'This creature if it survives will break up downs; if it is rent asunder will

5. By Albert S. Cook and C. B. Tinker, 1902, 1926; Cosette Faust and Stith Thompson, 1918; J. Duncan Spaeth, 1920; Robert K. Gordon, 1926; Charles W. Kennedy, 1943. Also by Stopford Brooke in his *History of Early English Literature to the Accession of King Alfred*, 1892, and in *English Literature from the Beginning to the Norman Conquest*, 1898.

bind the living' [i.e., if the suckling lives to grow up it will draw the plow; if it dies its hide will make thongs.]"

Number 22 (K-D 8), one of the best, is a more difficult example. First a literal, line-by-line version:

> *I through my mouth speak   in many tongues*
> *with skills I sing   change enough [often]*
> *in head-tone [or mourning tone]   loud chirm [cry out]*
> *hold my tunes [or customs]   voice restrain not.*
> *Old evening-scop   to earls [princes] bring*
> *bliss in burgs [towns].   Then I bending [varying]*
> *with voice storm [cry out]   still in dwellings*
> *[they] sit bowing.   Say what I am called*
> *who so clearly call   players' songs*
> *loudly imitate   to heroes bode*
> *many welcomes   with my voice.*

There are several uncertainties here which must be canvassed at the outset. First, the textual. In l. 3 *heafodwop(e)* means 'head sound'; Trautmann, a persistent emender, would read *heafodwope*, 'mournful sound,' and this would support the solution Wood-dove, Anglo-Saxon *cuscote*, which fits the text in other ways and was strongly urged by Dietrich. In the manuscript the rune for C stands above the text. In l. 4 *wisan* may mean 'tunes' (as in German *Volksweise*) or 'manner,' i.e., 'I hold (prolong) my song and do not sing out of tune,' *or* 'I sing according to my nature.' In l. 4 *hleoþre*, 'sound,' may be for *hleahtor*, 'laughter,' an emendation which receives some support from l. 9. In l. 5 *Eald* may mean 'old in years,' or 'of old,' in the sense of long familiar. In l. 8 the manuscript has *sited nigende*, 'sits bending forward'; *siteþ*, third person singular, is difficult and is changed to *sitted*, plural, by the editors: 'they [the earls of l. 5] sit.' For *nigende* (which Wyatt translated 'listening' in a footnote, but 'bending forward' in his Glossary) most editors read *hnigende*, 'bowing,' to avoid the repetition, *nige*, in the next line. In l. 9 the manuscript has *þa swa scire nige*. If *scire nige* are two words the meaning must be 'I listen brightly'; but most editors make it one word, *scirenige* (for *sciernicge*), 'female jester.' In the latter half of the line *sceawendwisan* means 'player's songs' or 'jesting songs.' Tupper cites *sceawendspræc, scarilitas* (for *scurrilitas*). Mackie translates: "who, like a woman jester, loudly mimic / the habits of a buffoon."

Thus l. 9 offers the greatest difficulty: the bird must be regarded as in some sort a joker. 'Player's song' may mean only something professional, but if 'female' is implied, together with the notion of scurrility, we have at least a vivid picture of popular entertainment. Mackie's "buffoon" may be a bit too strong.

Now, putting the pieces together, we have for the solution a bird which sings in the evening with great skill and various tunes, and also impresses the noble listeners with its serious music yet at the same time with something which is comic if not quite naughty. The welcome things of the last line may signify not pleasant tidings but merely singing which they enjoy. What bird meets all the requirements? The probabilities are about equally divided, among the commentators, between Nightingale and some kind of Jay or Jackdaw, and neither is wholly satisfactory. Hence this seems to be one of those riddles which are intended to provoke argument or indecisive discussion. The uncertainties are part of the fun.

It goes without saying that this has been a trial to the translators, for a translation must be slanted to match the chosen solution. Some specimens follow. The first is in prose by R. K. Gordon, in the Everyman Library, and is headed "Nightingale or Jay":

I speak with many voices through my mouth, sing with modulated notes: often I change my voice, I cry aloud, I hold my melody, nor do I refrain from laughter. Aged bard of the evening, I bring to men joy in cities when I cry with varying voice; they sit in silence, quiet in the dwellings. Say what my name is who, like a female jester, loudly mimic a player's song, announce to men many welcome things with my voice.

The next is from Faust and Thompson, *Old English Poems*:

A Nightingale

With my mouth I am master   of many a language;
Cunningly I carol;   I discourse full oft
In melodious lays;   loud do I call

Ever mindful of melody,   undiminished in voice.
An old evening-scop,   to earls I bring
Solace in cities;   when, skillful in music
My voice I raise,   restful at home
They sit in silence.   Say what is my name,
That call so clearly   and cleverly imitate
The song of the scop,   and sing unto men
Words full of welcome   with my wonderful voice.

The next by Charles W. Kennedy, from *The Earliest English Poetry*;

I carol my song   in many a cadence,
With modulation   and change of note.
Clearly I call,   keeping the melody,
An old evening-singer   unceasing in song,
To earls in their houses   I bring great bliss;
When I chant my carols   in varying strains,
Men sit in their dwellings   silent and still.
Say what I'm called   who mimic so clearly
The songs of a jester,   and sing to the world
Many a melody   welcome to men.

(Professor Kennedy accepts the solution of Jean Young (*R.E.S.*, July, 1942), Song-thrush (*Turdus Philomelos Clarkei*).

Now an alternative rendering to that on p. 22 below:

Through my mouth I speak   with many voices.
I sing with cunning,   alternate often
high head-tones   and loud deep shouts.
I keep on the key   but with restraint.
Of old a nighttime   singer I bring
joy to the gentles   who dwell in towns.
When I raise my voice   with many modulations
they listen reverently.   What am I called
who cry out so clearly   with bright imitation

of professional entertainers   and bring with my singing
notes of welcome   to mortal man?

Or if less literal versions are wanted:

I speak a various language.
Loud I sing with notes ever changing
with professional skill always at evening,
long familiar to all good men.
They welcome my song. I bring them bliss
as they sit listening
at home with heads bowed in reverence.
Can you guess what my name is?

or

I speak very many languages well
And hold all good men under my spell.
I sing like a diva with coloratura
Loud and long with bright bravura.
They listen with joy and welcome my song
As they sit at home the evening long.
My notes are never twice the same.
You know me, and now you may say my name.

or

My tongue is tuned to many changing songs
With ever alternating shorts and longs;
With loud and low my old accustomed note
In cunning music issues from my throat.
I sing at eventide, and all who hear
Listen with eagerly attentive ear;
In reverent silence bowed they sit at home
Learning of many welcome things to come.
Attend and answer; try if you can tell
My name who mimic others' songs so well.

And lastly an adaptation by a poet, Lascelles Abercrombie (*Poems,* London, 1930):

The Nightingale
(From the Old English Riddle)

I through my throat   the thronging melodies
Delicately devising   in divers moods,
Let my little breath   lavishly chime,
Still the bestower   of unstinted song.
Of old to all men   my evening enchantment
Brings blissful ease;   they, when I bind them
With my thrilling sweet troubles,   enthralled in their houses
Lean forward, listening.   Learn now my name
Who cry so keenly,   such quivering glee
Pealing merrily,   and pour such musical
Ringing welcome   to returning warriors.

It is unnecessary to comment in detail on these renderings. Some of them strain to imitate the original meter, others are frankly rather free and avoid the textual difficulties. Professor Kennedy's is a careful compromise with the strict alliterative formulas, but ends by being almost too smooth, with concession to modern iambicism; and the choice of "carol" seems unfortunate because of the word's other associations. At least they point up the hazards and invite forbearance for the attempts which follow.

THE ARRANGEMENT

Orderly arrangement is not to be expected in a collection of riddles. Quite the contrary, insofar as they are meant to tease or test the reader, to group them according to the answers would offer too much help. Even the Latin *Ænigmata*, where the answers are provided as titles, are not placed in any definite order. In the first fifty-nine of the Exeter Book a few signs may be recognized. The Storm riddles have pride of place due to their merit; they are easily the showpiece of the collection. Then 7, 8, 9, 10 are about birds; 27 and 28, mead and malt liquor, come together but are well separated from 11, wine. No. 59, chalice, might have been regarded as a fitting Christian conclusion, but 40, creation, which Aldhelm placed at the end of his hundred is among unrelated subjects. The most markedly Christian riddles fall in the first fifty-nine but not side by side.

The six containing runes, 8, 19, 24, 42, 64, 74, are scattered. Of the seven "obscene" riddles five (25, 37, 44, 45, 54) are among the first fifty-nine; the other two, 61, 62, form a pair, like 44, 45.

For the present purpose of a non-scholarly edition, I have ventured, though with some misgiving, to bring together those of the riddles which are related by theme or subject, leaving a number which can only be classed as miscellaneous. To attempt a division according to merit would be risky, and by the distinction of learned and popular equally so. Even a grouping by subject is fraught with difficulties, partly because there is bound to be much overlapping and partly because of the variety of answers proposed by various scholars; and there are some which are still unsolved or *sub judice*.

The translations thus have each two numbers: the editorial number in parentheses and in the usual position, preceded by the new number. For convenience in cross-reference a comparative table will be found on p. 67.

ANGLO-SAXON RIDDLES OF THE EXETER BOOK

1. NATURAL PHENOMENA

The Storm riddles have pride of place not only because they stand first in the Exeter Book, but also because they outrank all the rest in poetic merit. After much discussion, the consensus now is that 1 is a separate riddle and 2 and 3 are a single riddle by a different author, in four parts and a conclusion. Thus 1 describes a destructive storm on land; 2, 3, divide as follows (*a*) 2, ll. 1-15, a submarine storm; (*b*) 3, ll. 1-16, an earthquake; (*c*) 3, ll. 17-35, a storm at sea; (*d*) 3, ll. 36-66, a thunderstorm on land; and (*e*) 3, ll. 67-72, a concluding review of (*a*), (*b*), (*c*), (*d*). The chief interest lies of course in the descriptions; the riddling element is merely, What produces the storms —are they from natural causes or are they of divine origin? Both authors reveal a knowledge of "Græco-Roman cosmology" (Plato, Lucretius, Pliny) and of mediæval theory (Isidore, Bede);[1] and the answer is, accordingly, not *which* but *both*. The Christian will say "God," the learned will answer "Natural Causes"; and both are right.

1 (K-D 1)

What good man is   so learned and so clever
that he can say who drives me   forth on my way?
When I rise up strong   at times furious,
I thunder mightily   and again with havoc
I sweep over the land,   burn the great hall,
ravage the buildings. Smoke mounts on high
dark over the rooftops.   Clamor is everywhere,
sudden death among men.   When I shake the forest,
the trees proud in their fruit,   I fell the boles.
With my roof of water,   by the powers above   10
I am driven far and wide   on my avenging path.
I bear on my back   what once covered the forms

1. For references see Erika Erhardt-Siebold, "The Storm Riddles," *PMLA* LXIV (1949), 884-88.

of the earth-dwellers,   their body and soul
together in the waters.   Say what covers me
or what I am called   who bear this burden.

A storm of wind, rain, thunder, and lightning on land. Ll. 12-14 refer
to the Biblical Flood.

2 (K-D 2)

Sometimes I set forth   —when none would expect it—
under turbulent waves,   seeking the depths,
the floor of ocean.   The sea is aroused,
. . . . .   foam is tossed up;
the home of whales   roars and rages.
Streams lash the shore,   violently dash
up the steep strand   with sand and shingle
and seaweed, when surging   I struggle and strive
beneath the sea currents,   stir up the bottom,
the broad sea deeps.   Nor can I escape   10
from the sea's surface   until He permits
who guides all my ways.   O wise man, say,
who is it drew me   from the sea's embraces
when the surges again   are stilled and quiet
and calm the waves   which covered me first.

(K-D 3, 1-16)

Sometimes my Lord   constrains me close
and forces me under   the broad bosom
of the fertile fields   and holds me there,
drives me into darkness,   where hard on my back
the earth sits heavy.   There is no escape
from all that torment;   but the houses of heroes,
their gabled halls,   I cause to tremble
and shake the walls   of the dwellings of men,
high over their heads.   The air seems still
in the skies above   and the waters quiet—   10

until from confinement   upwards I thrust,
even as He commands   who laid at the beginning
my fetters upon me.   I can never be free
from the power that points   the path I follow.

(K-D 3, 17-35)

Sometimes from above   I rouse the surges,
stir up the waters   and drive to the shore
the flint-gray flood.   Foaming the waves
fight with the wall.   Dim stands up
the dune over the deep;   dark behind it
blended with the sea   comes another surge.
Together they meet   by the sea-mark there
by the high ridges.   Loud is the wooden ship,
the noise of the sailors.   Calmly await
the steep stone cliffs   the battle of waters,
the clashing waves,   when high the violence
crowds on the headlands.   There must the keel
find bitter battle,   if the sea lifts it
with all its men   in that terrible hour;
till out of control,   robbed of its life,
it rides through the foam   on the back of the waves.
Then will be panic there,   manifest to mortals;
* . . . . .   but I must obey,*
strong on my fierce way.   Who will still that?

In this last there may be an echo of Matt. 8:24-27 (Christ calming the waves), and in the shipwreck picture a notion of divine retribution at the Last Judgment.

(K-D 3, 36-66)

Sometimes I rush   through the wan wet clouds
that ride on my back,   scatter them wide
with their streaming water.   Sometimes I allow them
to glide together.   Great is the din,

uproar over houses, and loudest of crashes,
when fiercely comes cloud against cloud
like sword against sword. Darkling spirits,
swift over mortals, sweat with fire,
with gleaming flame and fearful noises.
Above mankind with dreadful din   10
they fare fighting; they let fall then
swart rattling streams from out their bosom,
water from within. Fighting moves on
the terrible host; panic arises,
a mighty fear in the hearts of mankind;
horror in towns when gleaming shoots
the gliding demon with sharp weapons.
He is dull who dreads not these arrows of death;
he dies nonetheless if the true Lord
down through the rain, straight from above   20
lets fly the darts of the fiery storm,
its swift arrows. Few escape this
who are reached by the darts of the hostile rain.
I stand in the van of this battlefront
when on I press the column of cloud,
push through the strife in masterful might
on the breast of the burns. Crowding in battle
the high storm bursts. Then down I bend
under the helm of the sky close to the ground,
bearing on my back the burden I carry   30
by the command of him, the all-powerful Lord.

(K-D 3, 67-74)

Thus a mighty servant I do battle by turns—
sometimes under ground; sometimes I must deep
undermine the waves; sometimes from on high
I arouse the waters, or rising aloft
stir up the clouds. Widely I pass,
swift and violent. Tell me my name,

or who lifts and drives me,   when I may not rest,
or who it is steadies me   when I become still.

3 (K-D 29)

I saw a being   in wondrous wise
hold its plunder   between its horns,
a vessel of light,   of shining beauty,
bringing it home,   a spoil of battle.
It wished to build   a bower in the burg
and cunningly place it   —if so might be.
Then a wondrous being   came over the roof,
known to all children   of mortal men,
recovered the spoil   and then brought back
the unwilling exile.   Westward it went,   10
hurrying home   after the battle.
Dust rose to the skies;   dew fell on the ground;
night departed   and none thereafter
knew its way,   whither it went.

Some strange solutions have been proposed, but the correct one is no
doubt the monthly contest of Sun and Moon. The plunder is the old
moon in the new moon's arms. The moon would like to make itself a
home in the heavens, but the familiar sun comes up and the moon is
routed.

4 (K-D 39)

The books tell us   that this thing has been
among mankind   through many ages
clear and manifest.   A special power
it has much greater   than any men know.

It wishes to seek   all living beings
one by one;   then goes its way;
no second night   in the same place;
but homeless roves   for ever and aye,
the path of exile.   It is none the poorer.

It has neither foot nor hand,   nor touches the ground,   10
nor two eyes nor mouth   nor speaks with men.
It has no mind,   but the books say
it is quite the poorest   of all creatures
that were ever begotten   according to nature.

It has no soul nor life,   but makes its way
far and wide   through this wonderful world.
It has no blood, no bone,   yet gives aid and comfort
to many men   the wide world over.

It never reached to heaven,   it may not to hell,
but forever it must   live by the teachings   20
of the King of Glory.   Long is it to relate
how its way of life   will go thereafter
fate's crooked ways.

                    This is a marvelous
thing to say: it is all true
that ever with words   is told about it.
It has no limit.   It lives nevertheless.

If you can straightway   rede this riddle
with true words,   tell what its name is.

The usual answer is Moon and Day. The paradoxes remind one of
11 (K-D 40), with which it has some metrical and stylistic similarities.
Both may be by the same author. Mrs. von Erhardt-Siebold, who re-
gards it as "one of the finest" and praises its "ingenious and fascinating
poetry," offers the tempting solution (*PMLA* LXI [1946], 910-15) of
Hypostatized Death, in the manner of Plato. She divides it into seven
parts (as printed above): death is not real, not abstract; it comes
privately and only once; it is a "suprasensible entity"; it is not really
lifeless: it has eternal life; this is not conjecture, but fact; you first explain it and then name it.

5 (K-D 84)

A thing there is   strangely begotten,
furious and fierce;   runs a violent course,

rages grimly,   moves over the ground,
is mother of many   marvelous creatures.
Moving beautifully,   it is ever striving;
low-lying is its close grip.   None to another
can fairly with wise words   describe its features
or say how manifold   is the multitude of its kin.
Its ancient origin   the Father watched over,
beginning and end,   and his only Son also,   10
glorious child of God.   . . . . .

   . . . .

Mighty in strength   the mother is;
supported marvelously,   laden with food,
adorned with treasures,   precious to heroes;
her might is multiplied,   strength made manifest,
her face is honored   with happy usefulness;
a fair bright jewel   for the proud to wear;
cleanly and bountiful;   mighty in craft.
It is dear to the prosperous,   to the poor soothing,   20
goodly, excellent;   boldest and strongest,
greediest and eagerest—   treads over the ground—
of all that is grown up   underneath the sky
and that the sons of men   ever saw with their eyes.
So that glory weaves   the might of mortals,
although wise of mind   . . . . .
a man more knowing of heart,   a crowd of wonders.
Than earth it is harder,   than heroes older,
than gifts readier,   than gems dearer;
beautifies the world;   increases in fruits;   30
blots out crime . . .
often casts from without   a single covering
wondrously beautiful,   over all mankind,
so that throughout the world   men are astonished.

There were 56 lines in all, of which these are recoverable—some metrically dubious and obscure in meaning. The probable solution is Water
in its various forms and uses—if one has the patience to identify them.

6 (K-D 33)

A thing came marvelously   moving over the waves,
comely from the keel up.   It called out to the land,
loudly resounding.   Its laughter was horrible,
awful in its place.   Its edges were sharp;
hateful it was,   and sluggish to battle,
bitter in its hostile deeds.   It dug into shield-walls,
hard, ravaging.   It spread mischievous spells.
It spoke with cunning craft   about its creation:
"Dearest of women   is indeed my mother;
she is my daughter   grown big and strong.   10
It is known to men of old,   among all people,
that she shall stand up beautifully   everywhere in the world."

Iceberg, slow but deadly as it damages ships. The mother–daughter
relationship is simple: water into ice, ice into water.

7 (K-D 68, 69)

I saw the wight   going on its way.
It was splendidly,   wonderfully arrayed.
The wonder was on the wave;   water became bone.

Possibly Running Water, becoming ice in winter. The original has
wiht (wight), which may be a thing or a creature; and there may be
a pun in *wĕg*, with a short ĕ, meaning way, and *wēg* with a long ē,
meaning wave. Moreover, the scribe placed the usual sign marking
the end of a riddle after the second line as well as after l. 3; and further,
since the first two lines are almost the same as those of 72 (K-D 36),
q.v., it has been held that they represent the beginning of a riddle
the rest of which is lost. The third line alone would then be a riddle
by itself; which Tupper calls "admirably complete." Norman E. Elia-
son (*Philologica, Malone Anniversary Studies*, Baltimore, 1949,
pp. 18-19) has argued for a single riddle, describing Christ walking
on the water; but later he withdrew the suggestion.

8 (K-D 50)

A warrior is wondrously   brought into the world
for the use of lords   by two dumb things;
brightly extracted,   which for his hurt
foe bears against foe.   Strong though he is
a woman binds him.   He obeys them well,
serves them quietly,   if maids and men
tend him duly,   feed him fairly.
He exalts them in comfort   for their joy in life,
grimly rewards one   who lets him grow proud.

Probably Fire, the two dumb things (l. 2) being flint and steel.

9 (K-D 83)

Ancient my lineage   . . . .
I lived in towns   after the keeper of fire
. . . . .   encircled with flame
purified by fire.   Now earth's brother,
an enemy, guards me,   who was first for me
a bringer of sorrow.   Full well I remember
who in the beginning   drove my lineage,
destroyed all the world.   I may do him no harm,
but I raise up captivity   from time to time,
the wide world over.   I have many glories,   10
no little strength   in all the land,
but I must conceal   from every man
the secret power   of precious skill
and the path I follow.   Tell what my name is.

The text is uncommonly difficult, as though the author tried too hard to be "poetical." The answer must be Metal in some form: ore, gold, money. The keeper of fire is Tubal Cain (Gen. 4:22).

II. CHIEFLY CHRISTIAN

10 (K-D 43)

I know a noble guest,   dear to princes,
whom grim hunger   cannot harm,
nor hot thirst,   nor age nor illness.
If kindly the servant   always tend him,
he who must go   along on the journey;
safe and certain   they will find at home
food and joy   and countless kin;
but sorrow if the servant   obeys his lord badly,
his master on their journey;   nor will brother fear brother
when unharmed they leave quickly   the bosom of their kin,   10
mother and sister.   Let whoever will
with fitting words   name the guest or the servant
I speak of here.

Soul and Body. The guest is the soul; the servant, and brother, the body; they will both be harmed when they leave the earth. The mother and sister are the earth: mother since the body is dust, and sister since body and soul have the same father, God. This is a rather ambitious one, but metrically inferior. More often than is usually the case the word-order is determined by the alliteration. In l. 12 the guest is called "comer," apparently for the alliteration; in the last lines the alliteration falls on the weak words "or," "of." The first three lines read literally: 'I know a lordly dear to nobles guest in dwellings whom grim cannot hunger harm.'

11 (K-D 40)

Eternal is the Creator   who controls this earth now
on its foundations . . .   [and] holds the world.
Strong is the Ruler   and King by right,
mighty over all.   The earth and the heavens

He holds and wields   as He encircles them about.
Me he wondrously   made at the beginning
when at the first   he established this universe.
He bade me to live   long unsleeping
that I slumber not   forever after.
And me suddenly   sleep overcomes;   10
both my eyes   are quickly closed.
All this world   the mighty Lord
moves with mastery   in all its parts;
so that I at the word   of the mighty ruler
all this universe   encircle about.
I am so timid   that a fleeting phantom
terribly can   fill me with fright;
and I am everywhere   bolder than a boar
when swollen with fury   it stands at bay.
No banner-bearer   can overcome me   20
throughout the world   save God alone
who holds and rules   this high heaven.
My fragrance is stronger   . . . .
than any incense   or any rose
in the field of earth   . . . .
beautifully blooms;   I am stronger than that.
Although the lily   is precious to men,
and bright of blossom   I am better than it;
thus the odor of nard   I (quite) overcome
with my very sweetness   ever and everywhere.   30
And I am fouler   than this black fen
that here evilly   smells of filth.
All I govern   under heaven's expanse
as the beloved Father   taught me at the start,
that I must rule   with right justice
over thick and thin,   and everywhere hold
the form and feature   of every thing.
I am brighter than heaven;   the high King bids me
to hold and cherish   his secret treasures.
I scan all things also   under the earth,   40

the dirty dens   of evil spirits.
I am very much older   than this universe
or this middle-world   could ever be.
I was yesterday born,   a child begotten
to the glory of man,   from my mother's womb.
Fairer I am   than ornaments of gold,
although they be covered   with delicate work.
I am filthier too   than this foul wood
or this seaweed   that lies cast up here.
I am wider than the world   any and everywhere   50
and extend farther   than this green meadow.
A hand can seize me   and three fingers
can easily embrace me   all round about.
I am harder and colder   than the hard frost,
the grim rime   when it comes on the ground.
[I am] hotter than Vulcan's   up-ascending
fire and brightly   shining flame.
I am on the palate   of men sweeter
than the honeycomb   when filled with honey.
Just so am I bitterer   than wormwood is   60
that darkly stands   here in the forest.
Feed I can   even more mightily
and eat just as much   as an old giant,
and I always can live   a happy life
though I see no food   my whole life long.
I can fly more boldly   than the pernex² can
or eagle or hawk   ever could.
There is no Zephyrus,   that rapid wind,
that can anywhere   so boldly move.
The snail is swifter than I,   the earthworm faster,   70
the swamp frog   more active in movement
and the offspring of dung   is quicker in stirring,
which we call "beetle,"   when we give it a name.
I am heavier far   than the gray stone

---

2. An imaginary bird for Aldhelm's *pernix aquilis* (swift eagle). Chaucer, *House of Fame*,
III, 302, made partridges' wings out of Virgil's *pernicibus alis.*

or a lump of lead   which is not small.
I am much lighter   than this little bug
which walks on the water   with dry feet;
than the flint I am harder   which drives this fire
from this strong,   this hard, steel.
I am softer far   than the downy feather   80
that here in the wind   flutters on the air.
I am everywhere   broader than all the earth
and farther extend   than this green meadow.[3]
I encircle . . .   all round about
wondrously woven   with wonderful skill.
Under me there is   no other
more powerful wight   among living things.
I am above   the creatures all
which our Lord   did create
who can me alone   by His eternal power   90
restrain by force   from exceeding my bounds.
I am greater and stronger   than the large whale
which looks on the bottom   of the sea-deeps
with dim vision;   I am mightier than he
even as I am less   in my own strength
than the handworm which   the sons of men
in skilful manner   dig out with a knife.
I have on my head   no white locks,
cunningly curled,   but I am quite bald;
nor could I enjoy   eyelids or eyebrows.   100
But me the Creator   deprived of them all.
Now wondrously   grow on my head
so that they may   shine on my shoulders,
full wondrously,   curly locks.
I am bigger and fatter   than the masty swine,
the grunting boar   in the beech forest
that dark and rooting   happily lives,
so that he . . .   .

3. This line repeats l. 5 above.

This is a fairly close rendering of Aldhelm's hundredth and final riddle, *De Creatura*. The method is the same as that in *50* (K-D 35), q.v., which is based on Aldhelm's *De Lorica* and perhaps the same man was the translator: generally two lines for each of Aldhelm's hexameters—at least through l. 79. This use of two lines for one is responsible for the thinness of the style, as bald and unconvincing as the present version. For example, compare the opening lines of the Latin:

The Creator, who established the ages on eternal pillars, the Ruler of king-doms, who bridles the lightnings by his law, while the heights of the wide-spreading universe are swaying to and fro in space, formed me in various shapes, when in the beginning he founded the world. (Wyatt's translation.)

The Anglo-Saxon translator omitted most of the classical allusions, except Vulcan (l. 56) and Zephyrus (l. 68), but retained the word *pernix* (Aldhelm l. 35), which he obviously did not understand. Then beginning at l. 83 there are further examples of his misunderstanding of the Latin, which suggests that a different translator took over. Moreover, after l. 79 there are two lines not in Aldhelm and then a skip of Aldhelm's ll. 43-61, though some of the lines omitted are picked up at the end. Altogether, Aldhelm has 83 hexameters; Riddle 40 has 107 lines, having left out some 25 lines of the Latin, partly of course because our Anglo-Saxon text is incomplete.

12 (K-D 66)

> *I am greater   than all this world is,*
> *less than the handworm,   brighter than the moon,*
> *swifter than the sun.   All seas and waters*
> *are in my embraces,   and the bosom of earth*
> *and the green fields.   I reach to the ground,*
> *I descend below hell,   I rise above the heavens,*
> *the land of glory.   I extend far over*
> *the home of angels.   I fill the earth,*
> *the whole wide world   and the ocean currents,*
> *all by myself.   Say what my name is.*

This is plainly a condensed version of the preceding riddle, Creation.

13 (K-D 55)

I saw in the hall   where heroes drank
a thing of four kinds   borne in thither.
It was of splendid wood,   and twisted gold,
skilfully wound,   and part of it silver;
and the sign of the rood   of Him who raised us
step by step   up to heaven
before he stormed   the castle of Hell's people.
I can readily report   on the excellence of the wood:
there was maple and oak   and tough yew
and the dark holly.   They are all together   10
a help to good men.   One name they have:
Wolf-head Tree,   that often afforded
a weapon for its lord,   a treasure in the hall,
a gold-hilted sword.   Now show me the answer
of this my song,   whoever may presume
to say in words   how the wood is called.

This one is difficult, but the author liked it and called it a song (*gied*),
a poem. The solutions hesitate between Scabbard and Cross; probably
both are intended. A sword out of its scabbard may resemble a cross
and the Holy Rood was often described as made of four kinds of
wood. A wolf-head is an outlaw; the tree therefore a gallows. Altogether, a composite image—scabbard, sword, cross, Holy Rood, gallows on which our Lord was crucified. For additional complication
the verb translated "afforded" might also mean "warded off."

14 (K-D 30)

I am an active flame;   I sport with the wind,
enwound with wonder,   enwrapped by the storm,
eager on my way,   troubled by fire,
a blooming grove,   a burning flame.
Friends often pass me   from hand to hand
so that men and women   proudly kiss me.
When I rise up   they bow down to me,

many joyfully,   where I shall add
to the oncoming   of blessedness to men.

The first four lines give a free and fanciful picture of a tree; then by a conventional association the tree becomes the Cross. (See also the preceding riddle.) This solution was first proposed by F. A. Blackburn in *JEGP* III (1900), 4-7, and has been generally accepted with reservations about cup and harp. His translation is as follows:

> I am agile of body, I sport with the breeze; [tree]
> I am clothed with beauty, a comrade of the storm; [tree]
> I am bound on a journey, consumed by fire; [ship, tree]
> A blooming grove, a burning gleed, [tree, log]
> Full often comrades pass me from hand to hand, [harp]
> Where stately men and women kiss me. [cup?]
> When I rise up, before me bow
> The proud with reverence. Thus it is my part
> To increase for many the growth of happiness. [the cross]

In the first line "agile of body" is from the other text of this riddle in Exeter Book (f. 122b), where the variants add to the difficulties of translation but do little or nothing for the solution.

15 (K-D 48)

I have heard of a ring   bright without tongue
intercede for heroes.   Well it spoke
with strong words   though not loud.
This treasure for men   silently said:
"Heal me   helper of souls."
May men understand   the magic meaning
of the speech of the red gold.   May the wise entrust
their salvation to God,   as the ring said.

The solution of this pious little piece is Chalice. The word "ring" (*hring*) may signify any circular object, as in the following riddle.

16 (K-D 59)

I saw in the hall   a golden ring
which men beheld   with happy hearts,

with wise minds.   Peace and salvation
has God offered   to every guest
who turns the ring.   A word then it spoke,
the ring to the gathering.   It named the Saviour
of righteous men.   Dumb it brought
clearly to their minds   the Lord's name
and to the sight of their eyes   if one could grasp
the true meaning   of the noble gold.   10
The wounded Lord,   do as the wounds
of the ring had said.
Nor can to the prayer   . . .
the soul of any man   unfulfilled
seek the princely city,   the castle of heaven.
Explain how the wounds   of this splendid ring
spoke to mortals   when there in the hall
it was turned and revolved   in the hands of the proud.

"Who turns the ring" (l. 5) probably means: "Who passes it along."
Two lines are defective. They have been built up by emendation to
yield the meaning: "The prayer of any man being unfulfilled, his spirit
cannot attain to seek God's city, etc." (Tupper). Like the preceding
riddle on the same subject, this is not a success. One may suppose that
the pious author tried too hard.

17 (K-D 6)

Christ, the commander,   the true lord of victories,
ordained me for conflict.   I burn the living,
unnumbered mortals,   over all the earth.
I afflict them with pain,   yet never I touch them,
whenever my lord   bids me to battle.
Sometimes I gladden   the minds of many;
sometimes I comfort   those I make war on,
even from afar.   They feel it, nonetheless,
the hurt and the healing,   when now and again,
over deep tribulation,   I better their fortunes.   10

Above this in the manuscript stands the rune for Sun (*sigel* or *Sol*). The association of Christ and the sun is a commonplace.

18 (K-D 11)

My garment is darkish.   Bright decorations,
red and radiant,   I have on my raiment.
I mislead the stupid   and stimulate the foolish
toward unwise ways.   Others I restrain
from profitable paths.   But I know not at all
that they, maddened,   robbed of their senses,
astray in their actions   —that they praise to all men
my wicked ways.   Woe to them then
when the Most High holds out   his dearest of gifts
if they do not desist   first from their folly.

The solution is apparently Wine and a reproof of its excesses. Cf. *59* (K-D 27), Mead, and *60* (K-D 28), John Barleycorn. Ll. 5 ff. "I know not that..." seem to mean "it is no affair of mine that...." L. 9 has given trouble; probably "Woe to them when brought to the Last Judgment." Or "dearest of gifts" may mean the gift of salvation.

III. BIRDS

19 (K-D 57)

Over the hillsides   this air upholds
bright little creatures,   swarthy and dark-clad;
bold of song,   they fare in flocks
and loudly chirp.   They tread the headlands,
sometimes men's houses.   They name themselves.

Tupper calls this a "little swallow-flight of song," and gives Swallows as the answer; Trautmann (finally) and Mackie agree. Another guess is Gnats or Midges. The last words are ambiguous: either, as above, they have an onomatopoeic name, or "name them yourselves." The former supports Mrs. von Erhardt-Siebold's argument for Jackdaw, in *PMLA* LXII (1947), 1-8. The jackdaw belongs to the large family of *corvidae* and is relatively small (13-14 inches); its "song" caw is certainly descriptive, but the bird itself is hardly as small as the riddle implies. Wyatt meets various guesses with a proper sense of humor. To Trautmann's objection that swallows do not tread and gnats do not chirp loudly, he holds that "tread" is not to be taken too literally. "And, as applied to Gnats or Midges, I find it a perfectly delightful word for their up and down motion in the summer air." Whether they are loud "depends entirely on the distance from your ear. At his own selected distance. . . ." Still, Swallow fits the text better.

20 (K-D 9)

In those first days   my father and mother
left me for dead: there was no life yet,
no life within me.   Then a kindly kinswoman
faithfully covered me   with her own clothing,
held me and cherished,   kept me warmly,
even as gently   as her own children—
until beneath her,   as my destiny willed,

I waxed into life   with my alien fellows.
My friend and protector   nourished me then
till I grew and grew able   to go forth by myself.   10
Because of this now   her own dear children,
sons and daughters,   were fewer, alas.

Cuckoo certainly. The pleasure is not so much in guessing—we are
not asked to guess—as in following the double meanings.

21 (K-D 7)

Silent is my garment   when I tread the earth
or dwell in the towns   or stir the waters.
Sometimes my trappings   lift me up over
the habitations of heroes   and this high air,
and the might of the welkin   bears me afar
above mankind.   Then my adornments
resound in song   and sing aloud
with clear melody   —when I do not rest
on land or water,   a moving spirit.

Swan.

22 (K-D 8)

I speak through my mouth   with many voices.
Skilfully I sing   with many modulations,
loud and strong,   with various tunes.
I sing as I must,   unhampered, unhindered.
I am the nighttime   songster of old.
I bring joy to the men   who dwell in the towns.
When I sing out   with my flexible tones
they sit at home silent.   Tell me my name
who brightly imitate   professional singers
and loudly foretell   many welcome tidings.

Various answers have been proposed (see pp. xv ff. above), but the
most plausible (though it is hard to resist Nightingale for l. 5) is

Jay or Jackdaw. Some of the apparent inconsistencies may be intended to confuse the listeners.

23 (K-D 10)

My beak was close fettered, the currents of ocean,
running cold beneath me. There I grew in the sea,
my body close to the moving wood.
I was all alive when I came from the water,
clad all in black, but a part of me white.
When living, the air lifted me up,
the wind from the wave, and bore me afar,
up over the seal's bath. Tell me my name.

Barnacle Goose. There was a popular belief that it was born from a barnacle growing on wood, the plank of a boat, or a submerged tree trunk. Dr. Johnson's first definition of Barnacle is "A bird like a goose, fabulously supposed to grow on trees." The "currents" in l. 1 are literally a mountain stream.

iv. OTHER ANIMALS

24 (K-D 12)

I move on my feet,   I break up the ground,
the green meadows,   as long as I live.
If life leaves me   I then bind fast
the swarthy Welsh,   and sometimes better men.
Sometimes I give drink   to a strong man
from out of my bosom.   Sometimes the stately dame
treads me underfoot.   Sometimes the Welsh girl,
dark-haired slave   brought from afar,
stupid and drunk,   on dark nights
lifts me and presses me,   soaks me in water,   10
warms me sometimes   kindly by the fire,
her wanton hands   thrust in my bosom;
turning often   sweeps through the dark.
Say what my name is   who living ravage
the land, and dead   am of service to men.

Leather; first on the living ox, then made into thongs, wine bottles, and shoes, which are cleaned by the Welsh slave. But "sweeps" in l. 13 is Chaucer's word *swive* and probably carries a salacious innuendo.

25 (K-D 72)

[The first few lines are defective.]
I was little . . .   . . . my sister fed me. . . .
Often I tugged   at four dear brothers,
each one gave me   daily to drink,
through a hole freely.   I throve happily
until I was older   and left all that
to the swarthy herdsman.   I traveled farther
to the Welsh marches,   traversed the moors,
bound under a beam.   I had a ring on my neck,

suffered woes on my way,   was forced to perform
my share of labors.   Often the goad hurt me   10
sorely on my sides.   But I was silent,
never spoke out   to any man,
if ever the pricks   were painful to me.

The young Ox, fed at its mother's dugs. It grew up and left the milk-
ing to herdsmen; later it was forced to draw a plow.

26 (K-D 38)

I saw the creature,   of the arms-bearing kind,
greedy for youth's joys.   As its due it let
four nourishing fountains,   brightly shining,
shoot forth noisily,   as is right and proper.
Then spake a man,   who said to me:
"The creature, if it lives,   will break up the hillside;
if rent apart,   will bind the living."

Bull calf. See pp. xiv f. above. "Arms-bearing" means "masculine."

27 (K-D 76)

I saw a woman   sitting alone.

Hen has been suggested. Or this may be first line of a riddle, of which
the rest is lost.

28 (K-D 13)

I saw them, all ten,   treading the turf,
the six brothers   and their sisters too,
living and lively.   Their skins hung plainly,
visibly manifest,   on the wall of the house,
each and every one;   nor was any the worse,
nor side the sorer,   though thus they must,
despoiled of their raiment,   roused by the power
of heaven's Lord,   tear with their mouths
the gray-green leaves.   Their garment is renewed;

having now come forth   they leave their coverings   10
lying behind them   as they tread the ground.

This was best explained by Mrs. von Erhardt-Siebold in *MLN* LXV
(1950), 97-100. Ten Chickens, in Anglo-Saxon *ten ciccenu*, having six
consonants and four vowels. When they are first hatched their skins
cling to the broken shells. Then they begin to eat and are soon covered
with down.

29 (K-D 15)

My neck is white,   my head is tawny
and so are my sides.   I am swift in my stride.
I bear weapons of battle.   On my back there is hair
and the same on my cheeks.   Over my eyes
two ears stand up.   I walk on my toes
in the green grass.   My doom is certain
if anyone finds me,   if a slaughterous fighter
finds me hidden   where I make my home,
bold with my bairns.   And there I abide
with my little family   when the stranger comes   10
to my very doors.   Death is their doom.
I must carry them off,   save them by flight
with fear in my heart   away from my home.
If he crowds me hard,   moving on his belly,
I dare not abide   that fierce one in my burrow
(that would be surely   not a good counsel)
but bravely I must   with both hands and feet
create a path   through the high hill.
Easily I can save them,   my beloved kin,
if I can bring my household   by a secret way   20
through the hollow hill;   for there I need fear
never a whit   the murderous whelp.
If the hateful foe   follows me hard
through the narrow track   he shall have no lack
of the clash of battle   when we meet in the burrow;

when I get to the top   of the hill and turn on him
with weapons of war,   whom I formerly fled from.

Badger. The coloring is not quite accurate, but near enough, and some allowance must be made for evasive detail. The word *hildepilum* in l. 28 properly means 'javelins' or 'darts' and has suggested that the porcupine is meant. But the riddler has a good answer. He has loaded his lines with epic compounds—six of them hapaxes—evidently to create an atmosphere of heroic battle. When the badger gets into the open he fights the dog as man to man.

30 (K-D 77)

The sea fed me;   the water-helm was over me,
and waves covered me,   close to the ground.
I was footless.   Often toward the water
I opened my mouth.   Now people will
eat my meat.   They want not my skin.
When they rip my hide   with the point of a knife
. . . .
Then they eat me uncooked.   . . .

Oyster.

v. DOMESTIC SUBJECTS

31 (K-D 34)

I saw a thing   in the dwellings of men
that feeds the cattle;   has many teeth.
The beak is useful to it;   it goes downwards,
ravages faithfully;   pulls homewards;
hunts along walls;   reaches for roots.
Always it finds them,   those which are not fast;
lets them, the beautiful,   when they are fast,
stand in quiet   in their proper places,
brightly shining,   growing, blooming.

Rake.

32 (K-D 21)

My beak is downward   and low I move
and dig in the ground.   The hoar foe of the forest
directs my movements;   and so my master
goes bent over,   the guide at my tail,
drives across the field,   pushes me and crowds me,
and sows in my swath.   I go sniffing along,
brought from the woodland,   stoutly fastened,
borne on a wagon.   I have many strange ways.
I leave green on one side   and black on the other.
Driven through my back   there hangs beneath
a well-sharpened point;   on my head another,
firm and forward-moving.   What I tear with my teeth
falls to the side,   if he serves me well,
my lord who behind me   heeds me and guides me.

10

Plow, as would be easily recognized by those familiar with its struc-
ture. The "hoar foe of the forest" may mean the man who clears the

woodland for his field, the plowman, or the plowshare ("the iron which, in the shape of an axe, bears ill-will to the tree"). See B. Colgrave, *MLR* xxxii (1937), 281-83. The beak or nose is the plowshare; the wagon is the fore-carriage; the sharp point underneath is the coulter.

33 (K-D 91)

My head is forged with the hammer,
hurt with sharp tools, smoothed by files.
I take in my mouth what is set before me
when girded with rings I am forced to strike,
hard against hard, pierced from behind,
must draw forth what protects at midnight
the heart's delight *of my own lord.*
Sometimes I turn backwards my beak,
when, protector of treasure, my lord wishes
to hold the leavings of those he had driven 10
from life by battle-craft for his own desire.

Key. (Cf. also 75 [K-D 44], which is Key with a difference.) *"Delight"* is represented in the manuscript by W, the rune *wyn* ('joy,' 'pride'). Ll. 8 ff., "open the door so that the lord can stow the plunder of battle."

34 (K-D 58)

I know a thing with a single foot
doing deeds of might. It travels not
nor rides much, nor can it fly
through the clear air; nor does ship carry it,
a boat with nailed planks. It is nevertheless
useful to its master at many times.
It has a heavy tail and a small head
and a long tongue. It has no tooth;
part is of iron. It goes through a hollow.
It swallows no water, it eats nothing, 10
it desires no fodder. Often notwithstanding

it bears water aloft. It boasts not of life
or of gifts from its chief. It obeys nonetheless
its master's word. In its name there are
three real runes. Rād *is the first.*

Rād is the name of the rune for R and also means 'riding' (note also
"rides" in l. 3); in short, a Riding-well, or well with bucket and sweep.

35 (K-D 4)

Bound with rings   I must readily obey
from time to time   my servant and master
and break my rest,   make noisily known
that he gave me a band   to put on my neck.
Often a man or a woman   has come to greet me,
when weary with sleep,   wintry-cold, I answer him:
(their hearts were angry): "A warm limb
sometimes bursts   the bound ring."
Nonetheless it is pleasant   to him, my servant,
a half-witted man,   and to me the same,   10
if one knows aught   and can then with words
riddle my riddle   successfully.

A Bell speaks, calling the man who rings it servant and master; tells
how it rouses the sleepers on a cold wintry morning. The "bound
rings," e.g., is the "bell." There is something a little wrong in l. 8,
perhaps an omission which would make the speech clearer; and
"burst" is not normally transitive in Anglo-Saxon. Mrs. von Erhardt-
Siebold (*PMLA* LXI [1946], 620-23) argues for Handmill, and gives
a diagram.

36 (K-D 81)

I have a puffed-out breast   and a swollen neck;
I have a head   and a tall tail;
I have eyes and ears   and a single foot,
a rough hard bill   and a long neck
and two sides;   hollow in the middle.

My home is over men.   I suffer much
whenever he moves me   who stirs the forest,
and rains and hard hail   beat on me as I stand,
and frost freezes   and snow falls
on me, hollow-bellied   .   .   .   .

Weathercock.

37 (K-D 56)

I was in there   where I saw something,
a thing of wood,   wound a striving thing,
the moving beam   —it received battle wounds,
deep injuries;   spears caused the hurts
of this thing;   and the wood was fast bound
cunningly.   One of its feet
was stable, fixed;   the other worked busily,
played in the air,   sometimes near the ground.
A tree was nearby,   that stood there hung
with bright leaves.   I saw the leavings   10
of the arrow-work   brought to my lord
where heroes sat   over their drinks.

The favored solution is Weaver's Loom. The "striving thing" is the web still in the loom; it is injured by the needle or shuttle passing through it. The spears or darts "must be the teeth of a batten penetrating through the warp." "The two feet can only be the weighted ends of the two rows of warp threads." The tree with leaves is a distaff, with flax on it; and the standing warp explains the metaphor of feet. On this see the learned and well-documented article by Erika von Erhardt-Siebold, "The Old English Loom Riddles," *Philologica, Malone Anniversary Studies*, Baltimore, 1949, pp. 9-17. Mrs. von Erhardt-Siebold includes with the Loom Riddles 50 (K-D 35), Coat of Mail, which is related insofar as chain mail resembles weaving; and 45 (K-D 70), which is usually solved as Reed Pipe (p. 37 below).

38 (K-D 49)

I know a something   that stands firm on the ground,
deaf and dumb,   that by day often swallows
from the servant's hand   useful gifts.
Sometimes in the towns   the dark thane,
swarthy and dun-faced,   sends more of these
into its mouth,   dearer than gold,
which men of rank   often desire,
kings and queens.   I will not now yet
name his nature   who for use and profit
of doughty men   makes what the dumb thing   10
(that dun-faced nitwit)   first swallows up.

Probably Bake-oven; but Bookcase has been proposed. Perhaps both,
for the sake of promoting argument.

39 (K-D 65)

I was alive but said nothing; even so I die.
Back I came before I was. Everyone plunders me,
keeps me confined,   and shears my head,
bites my bare body,   breaks my sprouts.
No man I bite   unless he bites me;
many there are   who do bite me.

Onion. Cf. 74 (K-D 25), which is also Onion with salacious overtones.

VI. WRITING

40 (K-D 51)

I saw four things   in beautiful fashion
journeying together.   Dark were their tracks,
the path very black.   Swift was its moving,
faster than birds   it flew through the air,
dove under the wave.   Labored unresting
the fighting warrior   who showed them the way,
all of the four,   over plated gold.

Quill-pen. The four things are two fingers, thumb, and quill (or as in parallel riddles three fingers and pen). "Its" (l. 3) shows that the "four things" were a unit. The quill *qua* pen does not move faster than birds, but the expression is an allowable hyperbole, or even an example of synthetic imagery, with possibly a humorous glance at the deliberation of some scribes. Similarly, the warrior is the guiding arm of the scribe. The "plated gold" has been explained as "the gold mount of the ink-horn."

41 (K-D 60)

I was along the sand,   near the sea-wall,
at the water's edge,   and firmly fixed
in the place of my birth.   Few men there were
who looked upon   my home of solitude.
But at every dawn   the dark waves held me
in their watery embrace.   Little did I think
that ever I should   sooner or later
speak without mouth   over the mead-bench,
exchange words.   That is a kind of wonder,
curious for the minds   of such as understand not
how the point of a knife   and a right hand
and a prince's thought   and the point itself

10

purposely fashioned it,   that I with thee
should boldly declare,   for us two alone,
a spoken message,   so that no other men
should further grasp   the words of our speech.

Reed-pen or Reed-staff (*Runenstab*, a piece of wood on which the runes were incised); more specifically, according to B. Colgrave and B. M. Griffiths (*MLR* iii [1936], 545-47), kelp-weed (*Laminaria digitata*), an alga with a thick stem, easily incised, which, after being dried, can be re-wet to make the markings visible. Two facts, however, have given rise to an uncertainty; for references, see the notes in Krapp-Dobbie. First, it is unusual for a riddle to carry a secret message "for us two alone"; and second, this riddle is followed immediately in the manuscript by a poem of fifty-five lines called *The Lover's Message*, which begins: "Now I will speak to you apart," and goes on to tell how he was driven into exile and now is waiting for her to join him in the spring, when they can renew their vows of love. The poem ends with five runes testifying to his faithfulness; or they may contain the lover's name as a signature. Just after this comes in the manuscript a new poem, *The Ruin*, and then the final group of riddles (K-D 61-95). Thus it looks as though the compiler from whose copy the Exeter scribe worked had rightly or wrongly taken 60 to be an introduction to *The Lover's Message* and perhaps made some adjustments in bringing the two pieces together, chiefly by omitting the conclusion. If rightly, however, this is not a riddle at all.

42 (K-D 47)

A moth ate words.   To me it seemed
a remarkable fate,   when I learned of the marvel,
that the worm had swallowed   the speech of a man,
a thief in the night,   a renowned saying
and its place itself.   Though he swallowed the word
the thieving stranger   was no whit the wiser.

Book-moth. Developed from Symphosius 16, *Tinea* or Bookworm: "A letter was my food, yet I know not what the letter is. In books

I lived, yet I am no more studious on that account. I devoured the
Muses, yet so far I have made no progress" (Wyatt's translation).

43 (K-D 26)

An enemy came   and took away my life
and my strength also   in the world; then wetted me,
dipped me in water;   then took me thence;
placed me in the sun,   where I lost all my hair.
The knife's edge cut me—   its impurities ground away;
fingers folded me.   And the bird's delight
with swift drops   made frequent traces
over the brown surface;   swallowed the tree-dye
with a measure of liquid;   traveling across me,
left a dark track.   A good man covered me   10
with protecting boards,   with stretched skin over me;
adorned me with gold.   Then the work of smiths
decorated me with strands   of woven wire.
Now may the ornaments   and the red dye
and the precious possessions   everywhere honor
the Guardian of peoples.   It were otherwise folly.
If the sons of men   wish to enjoy me,
they will be the safer   and surer of victory
and the stronger of heart   and the happier of mind
and the wiser of spirit.   They will have more friends,   20
dearer and closer,   truer and better,
nobler and more devoted,   who will increase
their honor and wealth,   with love and favors
and kindnesses surround them,   and clasp them close
with loving embraces.   Ask me my name.
I am a help to mortals.   My name is a glory
and salvation to heroes,   and myself am holy.

Book—Bible. First the preparation of the parchment, then the writing and decoration are described; then the manifold values of what
is written. "It were otherwise folly," l. 16 (literally: not at all stupid
punishment, penance), has puzzled the scholars. Proposed renderings
are "not the pains of hell" and "let no fool find fault."

VII. MUSIC

44 (K-D 31)

Beautifully made   in many ways
is this our world,   cunningly adorned.
I saw a strange thing   singing in a house;
its shape was more wonderful   than aught among men.
Its beak was underneath,   its feet and hands birdlike,
yet fly it cannot   nor walk at all.
Yet eager for movement   it starts to work
with various arts.   It often goes around
again and again   among noble men.
It sits at the banquet-board,   awaits its turn   10
till comes its time   to display its skill
among those who are near.   It partakes of nothing
that the men there   have for their pleasure.
Brave, eager for glory   it remains dumb,
yet it has in its foot   beautiful sounds,
a glorious gift of song.   Wondrous it seems to me
how this very thing   can play with words
through its foot beneath   adorned with trappings.
It has on its neck   when it guards its treasure,
bare, proud with rings,   its two companions,   20
brother and sister.   It's a great thing surely
for a wise singer   to think what this is.

It is a Bagpipe, pictured in the likeness of a bird over a man's shoulder, head down (its beak, the chanter, on which the tune is played) and feet in the air (the two drones, brother and sister, which make the continuous sound). "When it guards its treasure" (l. 19) means the bellows, when inflated.

45 (k-d 70)

It is a splendid thing   when one knows not its ways.
It sings through its sides.   Its neck is curved
and cunningly wrought.   It has two shoulders,
which are sharp, on its back.   If follows its fate,
when it stands by the road,   so handsomely there,
tall and bright-hued;   useful to good men.

This is explained as a Shepherd's Pipe. "It" (l. 5) is the pipe before it is cut. Mrs. von Erhardt-Siebold (see 50 below) places it with the Loom riddles.

46 (K-D 23)

Uuob *is my name   read in reverse.*
I'm a beautiful thing,   shaped for fighting.
Whenever I am bent   and there flies from my bosom
the poisonous dart   I am all eager
to drive afar off   the deadly bale.
Whenever my master   who shaped me that pain
loosens my limb   I am longer than before,
till I spit forth again   the death-blended bane,
that very fell poison   which erst I swallowed.
This that I speak of   leaves no man easily   10
if that which flies from me   should ever touch him,
so that perforce he purchases   surely with his life
that fatal drink,   a full atonement.
Unstrung I obey   no man, but only
when skilfully tied.   Tell me my name.

This is one of the best, and offers several possibilities for expostulation and reply. In l. 1 the original has *Agof*, which spelled backwards gives *foga*; and this *foga* is an older form of *boga*, 'bow,' as the reader is expected to know. (I have tried to suggest this trick by the form *uuob*.) In l. 9 the original has *ealfelo*, a word which occurs only here; it means 'all-fell' or 'altogether deadly.' L. 14 begins *full wer*. *Full* might be the noun meaning 'cup' (and is so glossed by Wyatt), that is, cup of poison; but it is here the adjective, 'full, complete.' *Wer*, which the reader would naturally take to mean 'man,' is actually short for *wergeld*, the legal payment for homicide. Thus the first word of the riddle, properly understood, reveals the answer, and the reader can then give his attention to the ambiguous description.

47 (K-D 53)

I saw a tree   with bright branches
stand high in a grove.   The tree was happy,
the growing wood.   Water and earth
fed it well,   till wise with time
it met with a change: it was deeply hurt,
dumb with bonds,   covered with wounds,
but adorned in front   with dark ornaments.
Now it clears the way   for a treacherous foe
through the might of its head.   By storm they plunder
the hoard together.   Eager was the rear   10
and active in aid   if the van met danger.
None could venture   in difficult places.

The solution is supposed to be a Tree, cut down, and made into a Battering-ram. The last lines are corrupt, the meter defective. Various emendations have been offered.

48 (K-D 73)

I grew up in a field,   lived where the earth
and the sky fed me,   till old in years
they turned me aside,   those who hated me,
from the way that was mine,   that I held while I lived.
They altered my fashion,   took me from the ground
and against my nature   made me bow at times
to a slayer's will.   Now in my master's hand

. . . .

cares for me well   carries me in battle
with skill by his will.   It is widely known   10
that I among the bold   with a thief's craft

. . . .

sometimes openly   against a fastness
I break forth where   before was peace.
Swift in movement   he turns in haste

away from that place, the warrior who knows
what are my ways. Say what my name is.

This is about all that remains of some twenty-nine lines. Supposedly
a Lance or Spear, first as it grew in the ground, then as made into
a weapon. "With skill by his will" is an attempt to represent *cræft on
hæfte*; *hæft* means both the 'haft' of the spear and also 'constraint,'
i.e., the spear is forced to fight.

49 (K-D 5)

I am a lonely thing,　wounded with iron,
switten by sword,　sated with battle-work,
weary of blades.　Often I see battle,
fierce combat.　I foresee no comfort,
no help will come for me　from the heat of battle,
until among men　I perish utterly;
but the hammered swords　will beat me and bite me,
hard-edged and sharp,　the handiwork of smiths,
in towns among men.　Abide I must always
the meeting of foes.　Never could I find　　　　　10
among the leeches,　where people foregather,
any who with herbs　would heal my wounds;
but the sores from the swords　are always greater
with mortal blows　day and night.

Beneath this the manuscript has the rune for S (*scyld* or *scutum*)
which gives the answer: Shield.

50 (K-D 35)

Me the wet ground,　exceeding cold,
first brought forth　from within itself.
Neither am I wrought　of woolen fleece
nor of hairs, with skill;　I know it in my mind.
I have no winding wefts　nor any warp in me;
nor with strong rods　does the thread resound for me,
nor the whirring shuttle　move across me,
nor the weaver's rods　anywhere smite me.

Worms do not weave me   with fatal wiles
which fairly adorn   the fine yellow web.   10
Yet nevertheless   the wide world over
one will call me a joyful   garment for heroes.
Say now truly,   you cunning sage,
learned in language,   what this garment may be.

In short, a Coat of Mail—woven, but not of wool or of silk. Weaving is suggested, yet with a series of exclusions to show that the thing is not what you would at first suppose.

51 (K-D 20)

I'm a wonderful thing   shaped for fighting,
beautifully dressed,   dear to my master.
Gay colored is my byrnie;   bright wire that my wielder
who guides me gave me,   embraces the death-gem,
who sometimes to strife   directs my wanderings.
Then I bring home treasure   through the shining day,
handiwork of smiths,   gold to the dwellings.
Often I slay   living warriors
with weapons of war.   A king adorns me
with jewels and silver   and honors me in the hall,   10
nor withholds my praise,   publicly proclaims
my merits before men,   when they drink their mead;
sometimes holds me back   or frees me when weary
with going into battle.   I have often hurt another
at the hands of his friend.   I am far and wide hated,
accursed among weapons.   I must never hope
that a son will avenge me   on the life of my slayer
if ever an enemy   assails me in battle;
nor will my kin be increased,   the breed whence I sprang—
unless bereft of my lord   I might change to a new,   20
turn from the owner   who first rewarded me.
Henceforth I am fated   if I follow a (new) lord
to do battle for him   as I did for the other,
for my prince's pleasure,   that I must forego
the wealth of children   and know no woman;

for he who held me   of yore in thrall
denies me that bliss.   I must therefore enjoy
single, alone,   the wealth of heroes.
Often foolish in my finery   I enrage a woman,
diminish her desire;   her tongue abuses me;   30
she hits me with her hands,   reviles me with words,
intones a curse.   I like not this contest. . . .

The solution is certainly, at first, a Sword, as is doubtless intentionally obvious. Then about midway the sword seems to be personified and obscurities set in. The piece is thus one half a transparent riddle and then a kind of heroic lay in the best tradition, in which the sword speaks as a follower who has somehow killed a friend of his master (or so I understand it) and is banished. He cannot marry, but he involves himself with a scolding woman. There is some disorder in the manuscript, the gatherings indicating the loss of a whole folio, which contained the conclusion of this riddle and perhaps other riddles. Compare *41* (K-D 60).

52 (K-D 17)

I protect my hearth,   my hoard and my home,
surrounded by strands   and filled within
with excellent treasures.   Often by day
I spit abroad   the terror of spears.
My success is the greater   the more I am filled.
My master sees this,   how darts fly from within me.
Sometimes I swallow   the swart dark weapons,
the poisoned darts.   My entrails are good,
precious to warriors,   the hoard that I hold.
Many remember   what goes through my mouth.

The manuscript has above this the rune for B, either for *Burg,* 'town,' or for *Ballista.* If the former, the answer is a Town defended by its inhabitants. Above the rune for B, moreover, is the rune for L, and this points to *Ballista,* an engine for throwing missiles, as the solution, favored by recent editors. Since both answers would fit, the ambiguity is probably intentional, to promote argument.

ix. HORN

53 (k-d 14)

I was an armed fighter. Now a young home-dweller
covers me proudly   with twisted wires,
with gold and silver. Sometimes men kiss me.
Sometimes with my song   I summon to battle
happy comrades. Sometimes a steed carries me
over the marches. Sometimes a sea-horse
bears me over waves   with my bright trappings.
Sometimes a maiden   fills my ring-adorned bosom.
Sometimes I must lie   hard and headless
stripped on the tables. Sometimes I hang,   10
with ornaments proud,   on the wall where men drink.
Sometimes a good weapon,   the warriors bear me,
riding on horseback,   when treasure laden,
I must breathe in the breath   of a man's breast.
Sometimes with my music   I summon proud warriors
to drink their wine. Sometimes with my voice
I rescue the booty,   put foe to flight.
*   Ask me my name.*

Horn, described under various aspects marked by the "Sometimes"
repeated ten times in nineteen lines: on the head of a steer, as war-horn
(also on ships), as drinking horn, as hunting horn, as warning against
thieves. "Ring-adorned," l. 8, 'adorned with a necklace.'

54 (k-d 80)

I am an atheling's   shoulder-companion,
a warrior's comrade,   dear to my master,
a fellow of kings. His fair-haired lady
sometimes will lay   her hand upon me,

a prince's daughter,   noble though she be.
I have on my breast   what grew in the grove.
Sometimes I ride   on a proud steed
at the army's head.   Hard is my tongue.
Often I bring   a reward for his words
to the singer after his song.   Good is my note,   10
and myself am dark-colored.   Say what my name is.

Various answers have been proposed, but doubtless Horn is right. The antler is made into a horn: it is filled with mead; its harsh note is heard in battle; it is given to a scop as reward for his singing. The first line of this riddle stands alone, K-D 79,

I am an atheling's   possession and delight

This may be a variant reading or the first line of a different riddle, of which the remainder is lost. For "note" (l. 10) the original has *wise*, either 'melody' or 'manner, way.'

55 (K-D 88)

Of the opening lines only a few words remain, and probably the end is lost.

But I stood upright   where I [was],
I and my brother.   Both of us were hard.
The place was noble   where we two stood,
the higher in honor.   The holt often hid us,
a shelter of trees   in the dark nights,
shielded us from showers.   The Lord made us both.
After us two large ones,   our kin will now follow us,
younger brothers   will drive us from our home.
I am unique in the world.   My back itself
is dark and wonderful.   I stand on the wood,   10
at the end of the board.   My brother is not here,
but brotherless now   I must keep my place
at the end of the board   and firmly stand.
I know not where   my brother is now

or where he dwells   on the bosom of earth,
who formerly dwelt   high by my side.
We stood together   in making war;
neither alone   declared his strength,
else were we in battle   both unavailing.
Now strange beings   tear into me,   20
injure my insides.   I cannot escape.
On the tracks he will find   success, he who seeks it,
. . . .   his soul's profit. . . .

Antler, horn, inkhorn. There is some disorder in the text apart from
the omissions due to damage to the manuscript; possibly the Exeter
scribe had an imperfect copy before him. Apparently the "tracks"
(l. 22) would be something written, homiletic or copied from the
Bible.

56 (K-D 93)

Text defective at the beginning and at the end.

Old with many days   over deep streams;
sometimes he would climb   the steep hills
up in his homeland;   sometimes he went back
into deep dales,   seeking for safety,
strong of stride.   He dug into stony ground,
frozen hard;   sometimes he shook the frost
from his bright white hair.   I rode with the eager ones
until my younger brother   seized the seat of joy
and drove me off   from my own home.
Then the dark iron   wounded me within;   10
no blood flowed forth,   no gore from within
though the sharp-edged steel   bit into me hard.
I mourned not the time,   nor wept for the wound,
nor could I avenge   my heavy fate,
a life for a life: but I suffer the torment
of all that bit the shield.   Now I swallow the black,
the wood and water.   I embrace within me

what falls from above   on me where I stand
(it is something dark). I have one foot.
Now the ravaging foe   plunders my treasure   20
who bore once widely   the wolf's companion.
What came from within me   moves on and on,
steps on the stout board   . . . .

The answer is Inkhorn, its history from its beginning as an antler to its use in writing. The lines are ambitiously elaborate and leave the impression that the writer's reach exceeded his grasp. A paraphrase will make the text clearer: "The stag on which I grew ranged the woodland, shed its antlers, and new ones grew in their place. The stag was killed and I was cut from its head and hollowed out to make an inkhorn. But I do not complain or seek vengeance, though I was sorely hurt by the iron instrument—what had, or might have, cut into battle shields" (or, as Wyatt interprets, "was pierced by the nails which fastened it to the stand"). The foe is the scribe with his quill pen (the feather of a raven, the wolf's companion in battle) writing on the stiff vellum.

x. MISCELLANEOUS

57 (K-D 16)

I war oft against wave   and fight against wind,
do battle with both,   when I reach to the ground,
covered by the waters.   The land is strange to me.
I am strong in the strife   if I stay at rest.
If I fail at that,   they are stronger than I
and forthwith they wrench me   and put me to rout.
They would carry away   what I ought to defend.
I withstand them then   if my tail endures
and the stones hold me fast.   Ask what my name is.

Anchor.

58 (K-D 32)

Beautifully made   in many ways
is this our world,   cunningly adorned.
Marvelous in its motion,   I saw this device
grind against the gravel,   crying out as it went.
This marvelous thing   had no sight nor feeling,
neither shoulders nor arms.   One foot only
had this curious device   to journey along on,
to move over the fields.   It had many ribs,
its mouth was midway.   Useful to mortals,
it bears abundance   of food to the people,   10
brings them plenty   and pays to men
annual tribute   which all enjoy,
the high and the lowly.   Explain if you can,
who are wise in words,   what this thing may be.

It is a Ship. Its one foot is the keel; the rest is easy. The verbal repeti-
tions are in the original. The first two lines are a formula, as in

44 (K-D 31), which just precedes it in the manuscript, and may be only a careless mechanical repetition on the part of the scribe.

59 (K-D 27)

I am honored among men   both near and far;
brought from the groves   and inhabited hills,
from vales and from downs.   By day I was borne
on wings through the air   and happily wafted
to the shelter of roofs.   Then they bathed me in butts.
Now I bind and I scourge   and I overthrow
the young to the ground   and the elders sometimes,
and this he soon finds   who takes me on
and attacks me with violence;   he falls on his back
unless he flees from his folly.   Robbed of his strength,   10
though strong in speech,   he is deprived of his powers,
and control of his mind,   of his feet and his hands.
Ask what my name is   who bind men to the ground,
the foolish after fighting,   in broad daylight.

Mead—the blossoming trees, bees, honey, stored to ferment, and then. . . .

60 (K-D 28)

There's a bit of earth   beautifully sown
with the hardest and the sharpest   and the grimmest that men
       own.
Cut and cleaned,   turned and dried;
pleached and wound;   bleached and bound;
adorned and arrayed   and borne away
to the doors of men.   Joy is within
for living creatures.   It delays and it stays
a long long while.   They live in joy
and naught gainsays.   But after the death
they start talking big,   chattering chittering.   10
It is hard for a wise man   to say what this is.

This is a sprightly companion to the preceding and more conventional riddle. It describes the preparation and effects of malt liquor and is sometimes given the title of *John Barleycorn*, after the much later ballad of that name. The first part is notable for its jingling rimes:

> *mid þy heardestan   and mid þy scearpestan* . . .   2
> *Corfen, sworfen,   cyrred, þyrred,*   4
> *bunden, wunden,   blæced, wæced* . . .
> *cwicra wihta.   Clengeð lengeð* . . .   8

From l. 6 on the text is puzzling and something may have been omitted by the copyist. Literally: 'it (the joy) clings, lingers, of those who before were living; for a long time they enjoy their pleasures and nothing gainsays (them). Then after death they begin to talk variously.' This seems to mean that those who drink are happy and feel alive for a time; then they are overtaken, dead to themselves, and talk recklessly.

61 (K-D 86)

> *A creature came   where many men*
> *sat at council   with wise hearts.*
> *It had one eye   and its ears were two;*
> *it had two feet   and twelve hundred heads,*
> *a back and a belly   and two hands,*
> *arms and shoulders,   one neck,*
> *and two sides.   Say what I'm called.*

A One-Eyed Garlic Seller; or so it would seem from a hint in Symphosius 94.

62 (K-D 85)

> *Not silent is my hall,   nor I myself am loud*
> *. . .   for us two the Lord ordained*
> *our ways together.   I am swifter than he*
> *and at times stronger;   he is more enduring.*
> *Often I rest;   he must run on.*

With him is my home   all my life long.
If we two are parted   my death is destined.

Fish and River. This is based on Symphosius 12.

63 (K-D 22)

Came sixty riding on horseback to the seashore.
Eleven rode on stately steeds; four white horses.
However they tried they could not cross the water,
for it was too deep and the banks too high and the currents
   too strong.
So they climbed on a wagon, with their horses under the pole.
Then a horse bore them all, horses and proud men with spears,
across the bay and on to the land,
though no ox drew it, nor powerful slaves,
nor stout steed—neither swam nor walked
on the ground under the strange burden,   10
nor stirred the waters, nor flew in the air, nor turned back.
Yet the men crossed the stream
and their steeds also, from the high bank.
So they strode up on the other side bravely,
men and horses, safe and sound from the water.

This is a rather simplified rendering (in a somewhat different meter from the others) of what is known as a world-riddle, found in varying forms in the Orient as in the West. Being interpreted, the sixty men are half-days (days and nights) of a month and the month is December. The four white horses are Sundays and the other seven are the feast days of December (Conception of the Virgin, St. Nicholas, St. Thomas, Christmas, St. Stephen, St. John Evangelist, Holy Innocents). The opposite shore is January, the New Year. There are difficulties in all this, but the main interest is the puzzling situation more or less realistically described. A quite different solution is proposed by L. Blakeley, (*R.E.S.* n.s. 9 [1958], 241-52), who calls it "The Circling Stars," i.e., the constellation of Charles's Wain. The sea is the expanse of sky, the horses are the stars of the Wain, eleven of which are visible to the naked eye; sixty is a round number for the surrounding stars.

64 (K-D 46)

He sat at his wine   with his two wives
and his two sons   and his two daughters,
the beloved sisters,   and their two sons,
goodly first born.   The father of each
of these noble ones   was there and there also
an uncle and a nephew.   Five in all,
men and women,   were sitting together.

Namely, Lot and his two daughters and their two children, Moab and Ben Ammi (Gen. 19: 30-38).

65 (K-D 52)

I saw two captives   carried in the house
under the hall-roof;   sturdy were they both;
companions they were,   fast bound together.
Close to one of them   was a dark-skinned slave.
She controlled them both   by fast fetters.

This at least invites guessing: for example, two Buckets from a well, or perhaps Flail (the two captives being handle and swingle).

66 (K-D 74)

I was a young woman,   a fair-haired lady,
and at the same time   a peerless warrior;
I flew with the birds   and swam in the sea,
dove under the wave,   and was dead among fishes,
and I walked on the ground.   I had a living soul.

One guess is Siren; another Water. If the latter, one would rather say Rain: a gentle shower, a heavy downpour, in the sea its natural form (its life) is lost; a little imagination can see it as hail walking on the ground. A third solution is offered by Mrs. von Erhardt-Siebold (*Medium Ævum* xv [1946], 48-54), comparing Frag. 117 of Empedocles:

> Once I was a young man, maiden,
> plant, bird, and mute fish cast ashore.

This, of course, is not a riddle, but an expression of cyclic metamorphosis. Just how an Anglo-Saxon came to know Empedocles is not clear.

67 (K-D 95)

This, the last riddle in the Exeter Book, is unhappily the most difficult. The text is complete but almost certainly corrupt, and any attempt to translate it is only a desperate hope, even after the experts have done their best with emendations.

> *I am a lordly thing,   known to nobles,*
> *and often I rest,   famous among peoples,*
> *the mighty and the lowly;   I travel widely*
> *and to me first a stranger   remains to my friends*
> *the delight of plunderers,   if I am to have*
> *success in the cities   or bright reward.*
> *Now wise men   exceedingly love*
> *my presence.   To many I shall*
> *declare wisdom.   There they speak not,*
> *none the world over.   Though now the sons of men*
> *who live on the earth   eagerly seek*
> *the tracks that I make.   I sometimes conceal*
> *those paths of mine   from all mankind.*

Perhaps Moon, perhaps Wandering Minstrel, perhaps Riddle. If the last, this is "a kind of monkish colophon to the collection" (Wyatt). Mrs. von Erhardt-Siebold (*MLN* LXII [1947], 558-59), taking "the delight of plunders" as a kenning for Quill-pen, would make that a clue to the solution.

xi. RUNES

Runic writing was brought to England from the Continent in the fifth century and ceased to be used after the Danish invasion of 866. The word *rūn* early took on a sense of mystery—as in *The Wanderer* iii, *gesæt him sundor æt rune* ('sat apart in secret communing'). Cynewulf used runes as a kind of code signature. In the Riddles they serve as a test of knowledge, as much as to say: I give you the clues in this form instead of by ambiguous description.

68 (K-D 24)

I'm a wonderful thing; I vary my voice:
I bark like a dog, I bleat like a goat,
I quack like a goose, I shriek like a hawk;
I imitate the eagle, the gray one, the cry
Of the fighting bird; sometimes the kite's voice
is familiar to my mouth, or the sea-mew's song,
where I happily sit. GIFT is my name,
OAK and RIDING and the GOD helps,
HAIL and ICE. Now you have my name,
as those six letters clearly betoken.

Here the runes are given their names, which of course are not intended to make sense; but their initial letters (underlined in the translation) are G A R O H I, which transposed spell HIGORA, jay or magpie. This is more like a puzzle than a riddle. If Jay is the solution of 22 (K-D 8), the two writers listened with different ears.

69 (K-D 42)

I saw there two beautiful creatures
openly playing the game of love.
If the affair prospered, the fair-haired one
proudly arrayed, received her due fulness.

> *Now I can tell   the assembled bookmen*
> *the names of both   in runic letters.*
> *There shall be* NEED, *two of these,*   N N
> *and the bright* ASH *tree,   one on the line,*   Æ
> *and then two* OAKS *and two* HAILS *likewise.*   A A   H H
> *Whoever has unlocked   with the power of the key*   10
> *the clasps of the chest   which held the riddle*
> *cunningly hidden   from the learned in runes—*
> *now is revealed to them   here as they drink*
> *how those two of low minds   are called by name.*

This is, as the author says, self-explanatory, if you recognize the runes: HANA (cock) and HÆN (hen).

70 (K-D 19)

> *I saw . . . S R O*
> *H high-spirited, with gleaming head*
> *running swiftly   over the fair land;*
> *it had on its back   warlike strength.*
> *N O M   rode not-mailed*
> *A G E W   far traveling it bore*
> *strong on its way   a bold C O*
> *F O A H   the course was the brighter,*
> *the journey of these.   Say what I am called.*

The first four lines are easy: S R O   H, or 'horse' written backwards, with an unarmed warrior on its back. The rest, five lines containing thirteen runes, is not easy. The text is certainly faulty and a great many emendations have been proposed. N O M is of course 'man.' A G E W for *wega*, 'of ways,' is genitive plural, but there is no syntax for a genitive. C O   F O A H is for *haofoc*, 'hawk.' Thus the general idea is: "I saw an unarmed warrior riding a spirited horse happily, with a hawk on his wrist." (See the following riddle.)

71 (K-D 64)

> *I saw W and I   going over the plain*
> *bearing B E.   For them both as they went*

was the owner's joy;   H and A
very strong.   TH and E;
the F and A rejoiced;   flew over EA
S and F   of the people themselves.

W and I is for *wicg*, 'horse': B E for *beorn*, 'man'; H and A for *haofoc*, 'hawk'; TH for *þeow*, 'slave,' or *þegn*, 'thane'; F and AE possibly for *fælca*, 'falcon'; EA for *ear*, 'ground' or *ea*, 'water'; S and P for *spere*, 'spear.' In brief: "I saw a man riding along on horseback with a hawk which was his joy (and pride). They were all happy, the man, the horse, the servant, and the hawk also; it flew over the water (or the ground)." F in the last line must be a mistake for P.

72 (K-D 36)

This riddle is somewhat related to the above, having a sort of secret writing instead of runes.

I saw a thing   moving over the waves [or *ways*].
It was gorgeously,   wondrously arrayed.
It had four feet   beneath its belly
[and eight man *hwm   wiif* mxlkfw
ƒ horse qxxs—up on its back.]
It had two wings   and twelve eyes
and six heads.   Tell what it was.
It moved over the water;   nor was it a bird alone,
but there was a likeness   of each of these:
a horse and a man,   a dog and a bird,   10
and also the shape of a woman.   You know
how to say, if you can,   who know the truth,
just how the nature   of the thing may go.

This looks at first like two different riddles; for it is not usual to solicit the answer twice. The two bracketed lines (4-5) are doubtless an interpolation by some overzealous copyist, to make everything more difficult. He used the simple old code of representing vowels by the alphabetically following consonants. Thus *hwm* (miscopied) is for *homo*, 'man,' repeating *man*; *mxlkfw ƒ* (also miscopied) is for *mulier*,

repeating *wiif*, 'woman'; *qxxs* is for *equus*, 'horse.' For the rest, inter-
pretations vary. Trautmann, for example, has the following: "A man
and his wife are seated on a horse; the man has a bird in his hand, the
woman a dog on her arm and an unborn child inside her (or the man
has the dog and the woman has the bird). The four feet are the
horse's; the eight on its back are the child's, the bird's, and the dog's.
The feet of the man and wife are not counted since they are neither
underneath nor up above. The six heads and twelve eyes are those of
those of the man, woman, child, dog, bird, horse." But he admits
that difficulties remain. Another guess sees a boat with four oars and
eight rowers and on board a horse, a man, a woman, a bird, and a
dog. Or no bird, the wings being sails. A more elaborate interpretation is proposed by Erika von Erhardt-Siebold (*PMLA* LXIII [1948],
3-6). A party of hunters is returning home in a boat with two dogs
and the game. The boat had four feet underneath (four oars) and
eight above (four oarsmen); the boat had two wings (bird being a
conventional metaphor for ship). The twelve eyes were those of the
four oarsmen, the dog, and the bird which had been killed. Besides
this there was the likeness of a horse (now the boat itself) and a
man (as on horseback), and a dog and bird literally. The form of a
woman is probably an ornamental design or figurehead of the boat.
Thus Mrs. von Erhardt-Siebold with slight changes.

73 (K-D 75)

Another one consists of two lines, the first of which says

I saw a swift one   going along the path

and the second consists of four runes: D N L H, which have been
interpreted as *HæLeND* or Savior; or with one emendation, D N U H,
i.e., *hund*, dog. (Note the other one-line riddle, *28* (K-D 76) and also
7 (K-D 68, 69).

XII. THE 'OBSCENE' RIDDLES

Obscene is a troublesome word for both legal and lay minds, but there is nothing uncertain about these few Anglo-Saxon riddles which go under that name. Most of the editors have been shy about their double meanings. Tupper, for example, puts the matter delicately, saying of 74 below, that the solution is not "the chief concern of the jest." Their interest today is as specimens of primitive humor sheltered behind the natural ambiguity of all riddles, which found a place in that book which the Bishop donated to his cathedral library.

74 (K-D 25)

I'm a wonderful thing, a joy to women,
to neighbors useful. I injure no one
who lives in a village save only my slayer.
I stand up high and steep over the bed;
underneath I'm shaggy. Sometimes ventures
a young and handsome peasant's daughter,
a maiden proud, to lay hold on me.
She seizes me, red, plunders my head,
fixes on me fast, feels straightway
what meeting me means when she thus approaches,
a curly-haired woman. Wet is that eye.

The pretended answer is Onion. Compare 39 (K-D 65), which is Onion only.

75 (K-D 44)

Splendidly it hangs by a man's thigh,
under the master's cloak. In front is a hole.
It is stiff and hard; it has a goodly place.
When the young man his own garment
lifts over his knee, he wishes to visit

with the head of what hangs   the familiar hole
he had often filled   with its equal length.

This is an inferior piece, meant only for its impropriety. The innocent
answer is Key. Compare 33 (K-D 89), which is Key *pure et simple*.

76 (K-D 45)

I have heard of something   wax in a corner,
swell and pop,   lift up the covers.
A proud-minded woman   seized with her hands
that boneless thing,   a prince's daughter;
covered with her dress   the swelling thing.

The answer is Dough. The first line contains a primitive pun (Wyatt);
the scribe wrote *weax*, the noun, 'wax,' for *weaxan*, the infinitive, 'to
increase.'

77 (K-D 54)

A youth came along   to where he knew
she stood in a corner.   Forth he strode,
a vigorous young man,   lifted up her own
dress with his hands,   thrust under her girdle
something stiff   as she stood there;
worked his will;   both of them shook.
A thane hurried up,   useful at times,
a capable servant;   nonetheless he grew tired
from time to time,   though strong at first,
weary with work.   Beneath the girdle
there began to grow   what often good men
love heartily   and buy with money.

The answer is Churn, Anglo-Saxon *cyren*, a feminine noun. This
makes for an awkward handling of the pronouns: "she" is too obvious;
"it" too misleading.

78 (k-d 61)

Often a goodly damsel,   a lady, locked me
close in a chest.   Sometimes with her hands
she took me out   and gave me to her lord,
a fine chieftain,   as he commanded her.
Then he thrust his head   well inside me,
up from below,   into the narrow part.
If the strength prevailed   of him who received me,
adorned as I was,   something or other rough
was due to fill me.   Guess what I mean.

The answer is an ornamented Shirt, which the man pulls over his
head. Up to a point this is innocent enough; but a twist at the end,
emphasized by the unusual formula, "Guess what I mean," conveys
the double entendre.

79 (k-d 62)

I am hard and sharp,   strong in entering,
bold in coming out,   good and true to my lord.
I go in underneath   and myself open up
the proper way.   The warrior is in haste
who pushes me from behind   a hero with his dress.
Sometimes he draws me out,   hot from the hole.
Sometimes I go back   in the narrow place—
I know not where.   A southern man
drives me hard.   Say what my name is.

The answer is Gimlet or Poker. "Southern" is a literal translation,
meaning perhaps a skilled workman as opposed to the cruder man
from northern districts; or one who works from below.

80 (k-d 37)

I saw the thing;   its belly was at the back
hugely puffed out.   A servant attended it,
a man of might.   And much had it suffered

when that which filled it   flew from its eye.
It does not always die   when it has to give
what is in it to another.   But there comes again
reward to its bosom.   Its bloom returns.
It creates a son;   it is its own father.

The answer is Bellows, but the second meaning is unmistakable. The
seventeenth-century play on the word "die" has thus a long history.
Symphosius 73 begins with an interesting, and innocent, parallel:

> Non ego continuo morior, cum spiritus exit;
> Nam redit assidue, quamvis et saepe recedit.

81 (K-D *87*)

I saw a marvelous thing;   it had a big belly
mightily swollen.   A servant followed it,
powerful and strong of hand.   Great I thought him,
a goodly warrior.   He seized hold at once,
with heaven's tooth   . . . .
blew in its eye.   It barked,
weakened willingly;   would none the less

. . . .

The rest is lacking. This looks like a variant of the preceding riddle.
"Heaven's tooth," the bite of the wind, has been compared with *As
You Like It* II, vii, l. 177.

XIII. FRAGMENTS

Several riddles either incomplete or fragmentary, owing to damage
to the manuscript, require only brief description.

82 (K-D 18)

I'm a wonderful thing,   cannot say a word
or speak for men   though I have a mouth
a broad belly   . . . .
I was on a ship   and more of my kindred.

There is no gap in the manuscript but the equivalent of a half-line,
and probably more, has been skipped by the copyist.

83 (K-D 41)

The riddle which precedes this in the manuscript, 11 Creation
(K-D 40), is left at the bottom of fol. 111b with an incomplete line,
and the one which follows begins at the top of the next folio also with
an incomplete line. It is obvious that a leaf was missing, or was over-
looked by the copyist. Thus we have only the last eight lines of the
original.

renewed
That is mother   of many kindreds,
of the best,   of the darkest,
of the dearest   that the children of men
throughout the bosom of earth   own with joy.
We here on earth   cannot live at all
unless we enjoy   what those children do.
This is something for all mortals   to reflect on,
all learned men,   what this thing is.

84 (K-D 63)

Often shall I prove   to be a thing of value
to the joys of the hall   when I am brought forth,
happy with gold,   where men are drinking.
Often in the bower   the faithful servant
kisses my mouth   where we two are together . . .

There were eleven more lines, now fragmentary. The answer is probably Beaker, with suggestive undertones. Tupper quotes a modern riddle in which Gill is used punningly for liquid measure and a girl's name.

85 (K-D 67)

I have heard   of a splendid thing,
of the Lord of peoples,   a word of incantation . . .

Several defective lines and then the conclusion:

I have become
a teacher of peoples,   live an eternal life
in many lands,   while men inhabit
the bosom of earth.   I have often seen it
adorned with gold   where men were drinking,
with treasures and silver.   Say if you can,
if you are wise enough,   what this thing is.

86 (K-D 71)

I am a strong man's property   clothed in red [gold?].
My place was first   the hard steep ground
with fair bright herbs.   Now I am the leavings of harsh things,
the fire and the file.   I am closely constrained
and honored with wires.   He sometimes weeps,
the bearer of gold,   because of my grasp
when I shall ravage   . . .

87 (K-D 78)

Probably eight lines, from which some twenty words remain.

88 (K-D 82)

Probably six lines, from which a dozen words remain.

89 (K-D 89)

Probably ten lines, from which some twenty words remain.

90 (K-D 92)

I was the boast of brown [things], a tree in the forest,
a fine living thing and fruit of the field,
a foundation of joy, a woman's message,
gold in the homes. Now I am a warrior's
happy weapon with a ring . . .

The rest is lost. Supposedly Beech tree (the brown things are swine, which eat beech-mast) and Book, then a treasure or treasured message, and finally a weapon.

91 (K-D 94)

Smith . . .
higher than heaven . . .
                    . . . than the sun
.   .   .   .
sharper than salt . . .
dearer than all this light, brighter than . . .

BIBLIOGRAPHICAL NOTE

There have been five editions of the Riddles in the last fifty years, and a number of learned articles—those which I have found most useful are cited in the appropriate places.

Tupper, Frederick, Jr. *The Riddles of the Exeter Book*, Boston, 1910. Pp. cxi, 292. The most elaborate edition, with a long Introduction, full notes, and a Glossary.

Wyatt, A. J. *Old English Riddles*, Boston and London, 1912. Pp. xxxix, 193. Small but with a good Introduction, spare notes, and a Glossary.

Trautmann, Moritz. *Die Altenglischen Rätsel*. Heidelberg, 1915. Pp. xix, 203. A condensed edition, with notes and Glossary.

Mackie, W. S. *The Exeter Book, Part II*. London, 1934. E.E.T.S. 194. Pp. 88-151, 190-91, 202-39. Text, with line-for-line translation on facing pages; no notes, no Glossary.

Krapp, George Philip, and Elliott Van Kirk Dobbie. *The Exeter Book*, New York, 1936. Pp. lxv-lxvii, 180-210, 224-25, 229-43, 321-52, 361 f., 366-82. Introduction, condensed notes, no Glossary.

NOTE: The editors have numbered the Riddles differently but all agree for Nos. 1-67, *except* that Tupper has the *Quondam First Riddle* as 1 and it is necessary to subtract one from his references; *and* Trautmann treats 1, 2, 3, as 1 and it is necessary to add two to his numbering. *Also* Trautmann and Krapp-Dobbie make two riddles of 68, 69. Wyatt omits the Latin riddle. Thus in tabular view:

Tupper	Wyatt	Trautmann	Mackie	Krapp-Dobbie
69	68	66,67	68	68,69
70	69	68	69	70
89	88	87	88	89
90	om.	88	89	90 (Latin)
91	89	89	90	91
92	90	90	91	92
93	91	91	92	93
94	92	92	93	94
95	93	93	94	95

With the translations above I have added in parentheses the numbering of the Krapp-Dobbie edition.

NUMBERING OF THE TRANSLATIONS
AND THE KRAPP-DOBBIE EDITION

K-D	Translation	K-D	Translation	K-D	Translation
1	1	33	6	64	71
2,3	2	34	31	65	39
4	35	35	50	66	12
5	49	36	72	67	85
6	17	37	80	68,69	7
7	21	38	26	70	45
8	22	39	4	71	86
9	20	40	11	72	25
10	23	41	83	73	48
11	18	42	69	74	66
12	24	43	10	75	73
13	28	44	75	76	27
14	53	45	76	77	30
15	29	46	64	78	87
16	57	47	42	(79	55)
17	52	48	15	80	54
18	82	49	38	81	36
19	70	50	8	82	88
20	51	51	40	83	9
21	32	52	65	84	5
22	63	53	47	85	62
23	46	54	77	86	61
24	68	55	13	87	81
25	74	56	37	88	55
26	43	57	19	89	89
27	59	58	34	(90	Latin)
28	60	59	10	91	33
29	3	60	41	92	90
30	14	61	78	93	56
31	44	62	79	94	91
32	58	63	84	95	67

INDEX OF SOLUTIONS